SHIMBA
BIBLE STUDY SERIES

THE DIVINITY OF JESUS

PROPHESIED BY ISAIAH

Dr. Maxwell Shimba

SHIMBA
PUBLISHING

TABLE OF CONTENTS

INTRODUCTION

The Divine Blueprint

The life and teachings of Jesus Christ form the cornerstone of Christian faith and theology. His presence in the world, His profound teachings, and His miraculous deeds have left an indelible mark on human history. However, the story of Jesus did not begin with His birth in Bethlehem or His ministry in Galilee. Long before these events, the Hebrew Scriptures foretold the coming of a Messiah, a Savior who would redeem humanity and establish God's eternal kingdom. Among these ancient prophecies, the book of Isaiah stands out as a beacon of hope and divine promise.

Isaiah, a major prophet in the Old Testament, lived and prophesied during a tumultuous period in Israel's history. His writings, filled with vivid imagery and profound revelations, spoke not only to the immediate circumstances of his time but also pointed forward to a future deliverer. Isaiah's prophecies encompass a broad range of themes, including judgment, hope, redemption, and restoration. Central to his message is the anticipation of a Messiah, one who would be called Immanuel, meaning "God with us."

In Isaiah 7:14, we find the remarkable prophecy: "Therefore the Lord himself will give you a sign: The virgin will conceive and give birth to a son, and will call him Immanuel." This prophecy was a promise of divine intervention, a sign that God would come to dwell among His people in a profound and unprecedented way. Centuries later, this prophecy was fulfilled in the birth of Jesus Christ, as recorded in the Gospels of Matthew and Luke.

Isaiah 9:6-7 further illuminates the divine nature and mission of this promised child: "For to us a child is born, to us a son is given, and the government will be on his shoulders. And he will be called Wonderful Counselor, Mighty God, Everlasting Father, Prince of Peace. Of the greatness of his government and peace, there will be no end. He will reign on David's throne and over his kingdom, establishing and upholding it with justice and righteousness from that time on and forever. The zeal of the Lord Almighty will accomplish this."

These titles – Wonderful Counselor, Mighty God, Everlasting Father, Prince of Peace – are not merely honorary. They reveal the multifaceted nature of the Messiah, who is both divine and human, embodying God's wisdom, power, eternal presence, and peace. Jesus Christ, in His life and ministry, exemplified these attributes, fulfilling the ancient prophecies and affirming His identity as the promised Savior.

The book of Isaiah also presents the image of the Suffering Servant, a figure who would endure suffering and rejection to bring salvation to many. Isaiah 53 is perhaps the most poignant and detailed prophecy of this Servant's sacrificial role: "He was despised and rejected by mankind, a man of suffering, and familiar with pain. Like one from whom people hide their faces he was despised, and we held him in low esteem. Surely he took up our pain and bore our suffering, yet we considered him punished by God, stricken by him, and afflicted. But he was pierced for our transgressions, he was crushed for our iniquities; the punishment that brought us peace was on him, and by his wounds, we are healed."

This prophecy finds its fulfillment in the passion and crucifixion of Jesus, who bore the sins of humanity and offered Himself as a perfect sacrifice. Through His death and resurrection, He opened the way for reconciliation with God, embodying the ultimate expression of divine love and mercy.

In this book, we will journey through the life and teachings of Jesus Christ, exploring how His actions and words reveal His divine nature and fulfill the prophecies of Isaiah. We will delve into the profound lessons He imparted during His ministry, lessons that continue to resonate and guide millions of believers today. From the Sermon on the Mount to His parables, miracles, and the Great Commission, Jesus' teachings offer timeless wisdom and a blueprint for living a life aligned with God's will.

As we examine Jesus' divinity, we will see how His birth, life, death, and resurrection align with Isaiah's prophecies, confirming Him as the long-awaited Messiah. By understanding these connections, we deepen our faith and appreciation for the divine plan that unfolded through Jesus Christ.

The exploration of Jesus' divinity and teachings is not merely an academic exercise; it is an invitation to encounter the living God. Through this journey, we are called to reflect on our own lives, to embrace the transformative power of Jesus' message, and to walk in the light of His love and truth.

Let us embark on this journey with open hearts and minds, ready to discover the profound depths of Jesus' divinity as foretold by Isaiah and manifested in the Gospels. May this exploration enrich our understanding and inspire us to live more fully in the presence of our Savior, Jesus Christ.

DR. MAXWELL SHIMBA

THE PROPHETIC FOUNDATION IN ISAIAH

The Sign of Immanuel

Isaiah 7:14 (NIV): "Therefore the Lord himself will give you a sign: The virgin will conceive and give birth to a son, and will call him Immanuel."

The prophecy of Isaiah 7:14 is one of the most significant messianic prophecies in the Old Testament, foretelling the miraculous birth of Jesus Christ. This prophecy not only points to the extraordinary nature of Jesus' conception but also underscores His divine identity as "Immanuel," meaning "God with us." In this chapter, we will explore the context, meaning, and fulfillment of this prophecy in the New Testament, using expository study and comprehensive commentary supported by Strong's Concordance.

Context of Isaiah 7:14

To fully understand the significance of Isaiah 7:14, it is essential to consider the historical and political context in which this prophecy was given. Isaiah prophesied during a turbulent time for the Kingdom of Judah. The threat of invasion from the northern kingdom of Israel and Aram (modern-day Syria) loomed large. King Ahaz of Judah faced immense pressure and fear, and it was in this context that God sent Isaiah to deliver a message of hope and assurance.

Isaiah 7:10-13 (NIV): "Again the Lord spoke to Ahaz, 'Ask the Lord your God for a sign, whether in the deepest depths or in the highest heights.' But Ahaz said, 'I will not ask; I will not put the Lord to the test.' Then Isaiah said, 'Hear now, you house of David! Is it not enough to try the patience of humans? Will you try the patience of my God also?'"

In these verses, God offers Ahaz a sign to confirm His promise of deliverance. However, Ahaz, lacking faith and fearing repercussions, declines to ask for a sign. Despite Ahaz's refusal, God declares that He Himself will provide a sign – the virgin birth of Immanuel.

The Virgin Birth

Isaiah 7:14 (NIV): "Therefore the Lord himself will give you a sign: The virgin will conceive and give birth to a son, and will call him Immanuel."

The Hebrew word translated as "virgin" is "עַלְמָה" (almah), which Strong's Concordance (H5959) defines as a young woman of marriageable age. While the term can simply mean a young woman, its use in this context, coupled with the miraculous nature of the sign, strongly implies virginity. The Septuagint, a Greek translation of the Hebrew Scriptures, uses the word "παρθένος" (parthenos), which explicitly means "virgin," underscoring the miraculous aspect of the prophecy.

Fulfillment in the New Testament

The fulfillment of Isaiah 7:14 is recorded in the Gospels of Matthew and Luke, where the miraculous birth of Jesus is detailed.

Matthew 1:18-23 (NIV): "This is how the birth of Jesus the Messiah came about: His mother Mary was pledged to be married to Joseph, but before they came together, she was found to be pregnant through the Holy Spirit. Because Joseph her husband was faithful to the law, and yet did not want to expose her to public disgrace, he had in mind to divorce her quietly. But after he had considered this, an angel of the Lord appeared to him in a dream and said, 'Joseph son of David, do not be afraid to take Mary home as your wife, because what is conceived in her is from the Holy Spirit. She will give birth to a son, and you are to give him the name Jesus, because he will save his people from their sins.' All this took place to fulfill what the Lord had said through the prophet: 'The virgin will conceive and give birth to a son, and they will call him Immanuel' (which means 'God with us')."

Luke 1:26-35 (NIV) provides further details: "In the sixth month of Elizabeth's pregnancy, God sent the angel Gabriel to Nazareth, a town in Galilee, to a virgin pledged to be married to a man named Joseph, a descendant of David. The virgin's name was Mary. The angel went to her and said, 'Greetings, you who are highly favored! The Lord is with you.' Mary was greatly troubled at his words and wondered what kind of greeting this might be. But the angel said to her, 'Do not be afraid, Mary; you have found favor with God. You will conceive and give birth to a son, and you are to call him Jesus. He will be great and will be called the Son of the Most High. The Lord God will give him the throne of his father David, and he will reign over Jacob's descendants forever; his kingdom will never end.' 'How will this be,' Mary asked the angel, 'since I am a virgin?' The angel answered, 'The Holy Spirit will come on you, and the power of the Most High will overshadow you. So the holy one to be born will be called the Son of God.'"

Immanuel: "God With Us"

The name "Immanuel" signifies the profound truth of the incarnation — that in Jesus, God has come to dwell with

His people in a personal and intimate way. This is a central theme in the New Testament and a cornerstone of Christian theology.

John 1:14 (NIV): "The Word became flesh and made his dwelling among us. We have seen his glory, the glory of the one and only Son, who came from the Father, full of grace and truth."

The incarnation is the ultimate expression of God's love and commitment to humanity. In Jesus, we see the fullness of God's character, His compassion, His justice, and His desire for a relationship with His creation.

Theological Significance

The prophecy of Isaiah 7:14 and its fulfillment in the birth of Jesus Christ hold immense theological significance. It affirms the divinity of Jesus and His unique role as the mediator between God and humanity. The virgin birth highlights the supernatural intervention of God in human history, setting Jesus apart as both fully divine and fully human.

Hebrews 1:3 (NIV) describes Jesus' divine nature: "The Son is the radiance of God's glory and the exact representation of his being, sustaining all things by his powerful word."

Comprehensive Commentary

The prophecy in Isaiah 7:14 was not just a promise to King Ahaz, but a message of hope for all humanity. It pointed to a future where God would intervene in a miraculous way, transcending natural laws to bring about His redemptive plan. The birth of Jesus, as recorded in the New Testament, is the fulfillment of this ancient prophecy, demonstrating God's faithfulness and the reliability of His word.

Matthew Henry, in his commentary, notes: "This prophecy, as it was to be accomplished immediately in Ahaz's time, it was a sign of the temporal deliverance of Judah from the two kings that were now coming against it; but as it had its accomplishment in the birth of Christ, it was a sign of our spiritual deliverance from Satan."

John Calvin, in his Institutes of the Christian Religion, emphasizes the importance of the virgin birth: "It was necessary that He who was to be our Redeemer should be God and man. It was also necessary that He should be born of a virgin, that He might be pure and spotless, free from every stain of sin."

Conclusion

The prophecy of Isaiah 7:14 is a cornerstone of messianic expectation and a profound revelation of God's redemptive plan. The virgin birth of Jesus Christ, as recorded in the Gospels, fulfills this prophecy and confirms His identity as "Immanuel" – God with us. Through His miraculous birth, life, death, and resurrection, Jesus has brought the hope and salvation promised in Isaiah to fruition.

As we continue to explore the prophecies of Isaiah and their fulfillment in the New Testament, we gain a deeper understanding of the divine nature of Jesus and the eternal significance of His teachings. In recognizing Jesus as the promised Savior, we are invited into a transformative relationship with God, experiencing His presence and love in our lives.

This chapter sets the stage for a deeper exploration of the prophetic foundation laid in Isaiah and its fulfillment in the life and ministry of Jesus Christ, providing a rich and comprehensive understanding of His divine mission.

Chapter 1: A Child is Born

Isaiah 9:6 (NIV): "For to us a child is born, to us a son is given, and the government will be on his shoulders. And he will be called Wonderful Counselor, Mighty God, Everlasting Father, Prince of Peace."

The prophecy in Isaiah 9:6 is one of the most profound and comprehensive messianic prophecies in the Old Testament. This verse encapsulates the birth, divinity, and eternal reign of Jesus Christ, providing a rich foundation for understanding His unique identity and mission. In this chapter, we will explore the titles and attributes of Jesus as prophesied in Isaiah 9:6, emphasizing His divinity and eternal role, using expository study and comprehensive commentary supported by Strong's Concordance.

Context of Isaiah 9:6

To fully appreciate the depth of Isaiah 9:6, it is important to understand the historical and literary context. Isaiah prophesied during a time of great turmoil and darkness for the Kingdom of Judah. The people were experiencing political instability, military threats, and spiritual decay. Amidst this backdrop of despair, Isaiah delivered a message of hope and restoration, promising the arrival of a divine king who would establish justice and peace.

Isaiah 9:1-2 (NIV): "Nevertheless, there will be no more gloom for those who were in distress. In the past, he humbled the land of Zebulun and the land of Naphtali, but in the future, he will honor Galilee of the nations, by the Way of the Sea, beyond the Jordan— The people walking in darkness have seen a great light; on those living in the land of deep darkness a light has dawned."

This promise of light and salvation finds its ultimate fulfillment in the birth of Jesus Christ.

The Titles and Attributes of Jesus

Isaiah 9:6 presents four distinct titles that describe the nature and mission of the promised child. Each title reveals a different aspect of Jesus' divinity and eternal role.

1. Wonderful Counselor

   - Strong's Concordance (H6382): The Hebrew word for "wonderful" is "פֶּלֶא" (pele), meaning "miracle" or "marvelous thing." The word for "counselor" is "יוֹעֵץ" (yo'ets), meaning "advisor" or "consultant."

   - Jesus is the embodiment of divine wisdom and guidance. His teachings and counsel are miraculous and beyond human understanding. He provides perfect guidance and understanding to those who seek Him.

   Isaiah 11:2 (NIV): "The Spirit of the Lord will rest on him—the Spirit of wisdom and of understanding, the Spirit of counsel and of might, the Spirit of the knowledge and fear of the Lord."

   John 14:26 (NIV): "But the Advocate, the Holy Spirit, whom the Father will send in my name, will teach you all things and will remind you of everything I have said to you."

2. Mighty God

   - Strong's Concordance (H1368): The Hebrew word for "mighty" is "גִּבּוֹר" (gibbor), meaning "strong" or "heroic." The word for "God" is "אֵל" (El), one of the names of God, signifying His power and strength.

- This title affirms the divinity of Jesus, recognizing Him as God incarnate. He possesses all the power and authority of God and is able to accomplish His divine purposes.

John 1:1 (NIV): "In the beginning was the Word, and the Word was with God, and the Word was God."

Colossians 2:9 (NIV): "For in Christ all the fullness of the Deity lives in bodily form."

3. Everlasting Father

- Strong's Concordance (H5703): The Hebrew word for "everlasting" is "עַד" (ad), meaning "eternal" or "perpetual." The word for "father" is "אָב" (ab), meaning "father" or "ancestor."

- Jesus is the eternal Father, indicating His timeless existence and paternal care for His people. He provides protection, provision, and a permanent relationship with His followers.

John 10:30 (NIV): "I and the Father are one."

Hebrews 1:3 (NIV): "The Son is the radiance of God's glory and the exact representation of his being, sustaining all things by his powerful word."

4. Prince of Peace

- Strong's Concordance (H8269): The Hebrew word for "prince" is "שַׂר" (sar), meaning "leader" or "ruler." The word for "peace" is "שָׁלוֹם" (shalom), meaning "peace," "completeness," or "welfare."

- Jesus is the ruler who brings peace. His reign is characterized by reconciliation and the restoration of wholeness. Through Him, we experience true peace with God and with one another.

John 14:27 (NIV): "Peace I leave with you; my peace I give you. I do not give to you as the world gives. Do not let your hearts be troubled and do not be afraid."

Ephesians 2:14 (NIV): "For he himself is our peace, who has made the two groups one and has destroyed the barrier, the dividing wall of hostility."

Fulfillment in the New Testament

The titles and attributes described in Isaiah 9:6 find their fulfillment in the person and work of Jesus Christ, as detailed in the New Testament.

- Wonderful Counselor: Jesus' teachings, miracles, and the wisdom He imparted reflect His role as the Wonderful Counselor. His words continue to guide and transform lives.

Matthew 7:28-29 (NIV): "When Jesus had finished saying these things, the crowds were amazed at his teaching, because he taught as one who had authority, and not as their teachers of the law."

- Mighty God: Jesus demonstrated His divine power through His miracles, authority over nature, and resurrection from the dead, affirming His identity as the Mighty God.

Matthew 28:18 (NIV): "Then Jesus came to them and said, 'All authority in heaven and on earth has been given to me.'"

- Everlasting Father: Jesus' eternal nature and His role as the sustainer and protector of His followers confirm His title as the Everlasting Father.

John 8:58 (NIV): "'Very truly I tell you,' Jesus answered, 'before Abraham was born, I am!'"

- Prince of Peace: Through His death and resurrection, Jesus reconciled humanity to God, establishing peace and breaking down barriers of hostility.

Colossians 1:20 (NIV): "And through him to reconcile to himself all things, whether things on earth or things in heaven, by making peace through his blood, shed on the cross."

Comprehensive Commentary

Isaiah 9:6 provides a profound and multi-faceted prophecy of the Messiah's identity and mission. The verse highlights the divine nature of Jesus, emphasizing His wisdom, power, eternal care, and peacemaking role. These titles collectively present a picture of a Messiah who is both divine and human, capable of fulfilling the deepest needs and longings of humanity.

Matthew Henry, in his commentary, observes: "This child is born to us; he is given to us, freely given, for the benefit of all mankind. He is the Wonderful Counselor, the source of all wisdom, the Mighty God, the embodiment of divine power, the Everlasting Father, the eternal provider and protector, and the Prince of Peace, the bringer of reconciliation and wholeness."

John Calvin, in his Institutes of the Christian Religion, writes: "These titles are not mere epithets; they are essential to understanding the fullness of Christ's mission and nature. As the Wonderful Counselor, He guides us into all truth. As the Mighty God, He saves us with divine power. As the Everlasting Father, He nurtures and sustains us. As the Prince of Peace, He restores us to harmony with God and one another."

Conclusion

The prophecy of Isaiah 9:6 offers a comprehensive and awe-inspiring portrait of the Messiah. Jesus Christ, in His birth, life, death, and resurrection, fulfilled these titles and attributes, affirming His divinity and eternal role. Understanding these titles enriches our appreciation of who Jesus is and what He has accomplished for humanity.

As we continue to explore the prophecies of Isaiah and their fulfillment in the New Testament, we gain deeper insight into the divine plan of salvation and the unparalleled significance of Jesus Christ. In recognizing Him as the Wonderful Counselor, Mighty God, Everlasting Father, and Prince of Peace, we are invited to experience the fullness of His presence and the transformative power of His love.

This chapter sets the stage for further exploration of the prophetic foundation laid in Isaiah and its fulfillment in the life and ministry of Jesus Christ, providing a rich and comprehensive understanding of His divine mission.

CHAPTER 02

THE MINISTRY AND TEACHINGS OF JESUS

The Sermon on the Mount

The Sermon on the Mount, recorded in Matthew 5-7, is one of the most comprehensive and profound teachings of Jesus. It encapsulates the essence of His ethical instructions and reveals the heart of His kingdom message. This chapter will explore the key lessons from the Sermon on the Mount, focusing on the Beatitudes, the Lord's Prayer, and the Golden Rule. Through expository study and comprehensive commentary supported by Strong's Concordance, we will uncover the depth and significance of Jesus' teachings.

The Beatitudes

Matthew 5:3-12 (NIV):

"Blessed are the poor in spirit, for theirs is the kingdom of heaven.

Blessed are those who mourn, for they will be comforted.

Blessed are the meek, for they will inherit the earth.

Blessed are those who hunger and thirst for righteousness, for they will be filled.

Blessed are the merciful, for they will be shown mercy.

Blessed are the pure in heart, for they will see God.

Blessed are the peacemakers, for they will be called children of God.

Blessed are those who are persecuted because of righteousness, for theirs is the kingdom of heaven.

Blessed are you when people insult you, persecute you and falsely say all kinds of evil against you because of me. Rejoice and be glad, because great is your reward in heaven, for in the same way they persecuted the prophets who were before you."

The Beatitudes introduce the Sermon on the Mount with a series of blessings pronounced on various groups of people. Each Beatitude begins with the Greek word "μακάριοι" (makarioi), meaning "blessed" or "happy" (Strong's Concordance G3107). The term signifies a deep, abiding joy that comes from divine favor.

1. Poor in Spirit: "Πτωχοί τῷ πνεύματι" (ptōchoi tō pneumati) refers to those who recognize their spiritual

poverty and dependence on God (Strong's Concordance G4434). Theirs is the kingdom of heaven, emphasizing that humility and reliance on God are the keys to entering His kingdom.

2. Those Who Mourn: "Πενθοῦντες" (penthountes) means those who grieve or lament (Strong's Concordance G3996). They will be comforted, pointing to God's promise to provide solace and hope in times of sorrow.

3. The Meek: "Πραεῖς" (praeis) signifies gentleness or humility (Strong's Concordance G4239). They will inherit the earth, indicating that true strength lies in humility, and God's kingdom belongs to those who exhibit meekness.

4. Hunger and Thirst for Righteousness: "Πεινῶντες καὶ διψῶντες τὴν δικαιοσύνην" (peinōntes kai dipsōntes tēn dikaiosynēn) refers to an intense desire for justice and moral integrity (Strong's Concordance G3983, G1372, G1343). They will be filled, assuring that God will satisfy their longing for righteousness.

5. The Merciful: "Ἐλεήμονες" (eleēmones) are those who show compassion and kindness (Strong's Concordance G1655). They will receive mercy, highlighting the principle of reciprocity in God's kingdom.

6. Pure in Heart: "Καθαροὶ τῇ καρδίᾳ" (katharoi tē kardia) means those with a clean and sincere inner life

(Strong's Concordance G2513, G2588). They will see God, suggesting that purity of heart leads to a direct and intimate relationship with the Divine.

7. Peacemakers: "Εἰρηνοποιοί" (eirēnopoioi) are those who actively seek to reconcile and create harmony (Strong's Concordance G1518). They will be called children of God, reflecting God's nature as the ultimate peacemaker.

8. Persecuted for Righteousness: "Δεδιωγμένοι ἕνεκεν δικαιοσύνης" (dediōgmenoi heneken dikaiosynēs) refers to those who suffer for their commitment to God's ways (Strong's Concordance G1377, G1343). Theirs is the kingdom of heaven, reaffirming that enduring persecution for righteousness aligns one with God's eternal kingdom.

The Lord's Prayer

Matthew 6:9-13 (NIV):

"This, then, is how you should pray:

Our Father in heaven, hallowed be your name,

your kingdom come, your will be done, on earth as it is in heaven.

Give us today our daily bread.

And forgive us our debts, as we also have forgiven our debtors.

And lead us not into temptation, but deliver us from the evil one."

The Lord's Prayer, also known as the "Our Father," is a model for Christian prayer that encompasses praise, petition, and confession. Each phrase is rich in meaning and theological significance.

1. Our Father in Heaven: "Πάτερ ἡμῶν ὁ ἐν τοῖς οὐρανοῖς" (Pater hēmōn ho en tois ouranois) (Strong's Concordance G3962, G2257, G1722, G3772). This address establishes a personal and communal relationship with God as our Father, who resides in heaven.

2. Hallowed Be Your Name: "Ἁγιασθήτω τὸ ὄνομά σου" (Hagiasthetō to onoma sou) (Strong's Concordance G37, G3686, G4675). This petition acknowledges God's holiness and expresses a desire for His name to be revered.

3. Your Kingdom Come: "ἐλθέτω ἡ βασιλεία σου" (elthetō hē basileia sou) (Strong's Concordance G2064, G932, G4675). This phrase calls for the manifestation of God's reign and sovereignty on earth, aligning human affairs with divine order.

4. Your Will Be Done: "γενηθήτω τὸ θέλημά σου" (genēthētō to thelēma sou) (Strong's Concordance G1096, G2307, G4675). This prayer seeks the fulfillment of God's purposes and desires on earth as they are perfectly carried out in heaven.

5. Give Us Today Our Daily Bread: "τὸν ἄρτον ἡμῶν τὸν ἐπιούσιον δὸς ἡμῖν σήμερον" (ton arton hēmōn ton epiousion dos hēmin sēmeron) (Strong's Concordance G740, G1967, G1325, G2254, G4594). This request for daily sustenance emphasizes reliance on God for our physical needs.

6. Forgive Us Our Debts: "καὶ ἄφες ἡμῖν τὰ ὀφειλήματα ἡμῶν" (kai aphes hēmin ta opheilēmata hēmōn) (Strong's Concordance G863, G2254, G3783). This plea for forgiveness acknowledges our sins and shortcomings, coupled with a commitment to forgive others.

7. Lead Us Not into Temptation: "καὶ μὴ εἰσενέγκῃς ἡμᾶς εἰς πειρασμόν" (kai mē eisenegkēs hēmas eis peirasmon) (Strong's Concordance G3361, G1533, G2254, G3986). This prayer seeks God's guidance to avoid situations that test our faith and moral integrity.

8. Deliver Us from the Evil One: "ἀλλὰ ῥῦσαι ἡμᾶς ἀπὸ τοῦ πονηροῦ" (alla rhysai hēmas apo tou ponērou) (Strong's Concordance G235, G4506, G2248, G575, G4190). This petition asks for protection and deliverance from evil influences and harm.

The Golden Rule

Matthew 7:12 (NIV):

"So in everything, do to others what you would have them do to you, for this sums up the Law and the Prophets."

The Golden Rule encapsulates the ethical teachings of Jesus in a single, transformative principle. It calls for proactive, empathetic behavior towards others, reflecting the essence of God's commandments.

1. Do to Others: "πάντα ὅσα ἐὰν θέλητε ἵνα ποιῶσιν ὑμῖν οἱ ἄνθρωποι, οὕτω καὶ ὑμεῖς ποιεῖτε αὐτοῖς" (panta hosa ean thelēte hina poiōsin hymin hoi anthrōpoi, houtō kai hymeis poieite autois) (Strong's Concordance G3956, G3745, G1437, G2309, G4160, G5213, G444, G3779, G2532, G5210, G4160, G846). This phrase calls for an active, positive approach to relationships, emphasizing mutual respect and kindness.

Comprehensive Commentary

The Sermon on the Mount presents a radical reorientation

of values, calling believers to embody the principles of God's kingdom in their daily lives. Each key lesson emphasizes the importance of inner transformation, ethical behavior, and a deep, personal relationship with God.

Matthew Henry comments: "The Beatitudes set forth the character of the true disciples of Christ, and the blessedness of possessing those characteristics. The Lord's

Prayer is a comprehensive summary of the petitions we should offer to God, showing our dependence on Him for all things. The Golden Rule is the sum of the second table of the law, guiding our conduct towards others."

John Calvin, in his commentary, writes: "The teachings of the Sermon on the Mount reveal the true nature of the kingdom of God. They challenge the superficial righteousness of the Pharisees and call for a deeper, heartfelt obedience. The principles laid out by Jesus are not mere ethical guidelines but are rooted in the nature of God Himself."

Conclusion

The Sermon on the Mount encapsulates the essence of Jesus' ethical teachings and provides a blueprint for living a life that reflects the values of God's kingdom. Through the Beatitudes, the Lord's Prayer, and the Golden Rule, Jesus calls His followers to a higher standard of righteousness, rooted in humility, mercy, purity, and love.

As we strive to live according to these teachings, we are reminded of our dependence on God's grace and guidance. The lessons of the Sermon on the Mount continue to challenge and inspire believers, offering timeless wisdom for navigating the complexities of life and relationships.

This chapter has explored the key lessons from the Sermon on the Mount, providing a comprehensive understanding of Jesus' profound teachings and their enduring relevance.

How the Teachings of Jesus Reflect the Principles Prophesied in Isaiah

The teachings of Jesus Christ, particularly those found in the Sermon on the Mount, resonate deeply with the prophetic principles laid out in the book of Isaiah. Both Isaiah and Jesus emphasize themes such as justice, righteousness, mercy, and the transformative power of God's kingdom. This chapter will explore how Jesus' teachings reflect and fulfill the principles prophesied in Isaiah, using Bible verses as references and providing an expository study with comprehensive commentary supported by Strong's Concordance.

The Spirit of the Lord

Isaiah 11:2 (NIV): "The Spirit of the Lord will rest on him—the Spirit of wisdom and of understanding, the Spirit of counsel and of might, the Spirit of the knowledge and fear of the Lord."

This prophecy speaks of the coming Messiah, upon whom the Spirit of the Lord will rest, endowing Him with wisdom, understanding, counsel, might, knowledge, and the fear of the Lord. Jesus' teachings in the Sermon on the Mount embody these qualities.

Matthew 5:1-2 (NIV): "Now when Jesus saw the crowds, he went up on a mountainside and sat down. His disciples came to him, and he began to teach them."

Jesus, filled with the Spirit of the Lord, imparts wisdom and understanding through His teachings. His counsel in the Beatitudes and other teachings demonstrates divine wisdom and knowledge.

Justice and Righteousness

Isaiah 9:7 (NIV): "Of the greatness of his government and peace there will be no end. He will reign on David's throne and over his kingdom, establishing and upholding it with justice and righteousness from that time on and forever."

Isaiah 42:1 (NIV): "Here is my servant, whom I uphold, my chosen one in whom I delight; I will put my Spirit on him, and he will bring justice to the nations."

Jesus' emphasis on justice and righteousness in the Sermon on the Mount echoes these prophecies.

Matthew 5:6 (NIV): "Blessed are those who hunger and thirst for righteousness, for they will be filled."

Matthew 5:10 (NIV): "Blessed are those who are persecuted because of righteousness, for theirs is the kingdom of heaven."

Jesus calls His followers to pursue righteousness and promises that those who do so will be satisfied and inherit the kingdom of heaven. His teachings underscore the importance of justice and righteous living, aligning with Isaiah's vision of the Messiah's reign.

Mercy and Compassion

Isaiah 61:1-2 (NIV): "The Spirit of the Sovereign Lord is on me, because the Lord has anointed me to proclaim good news to the poor. He has sent me to bind up the brokenhearted, to proclaim freedom for the captives and release from darkness for the prisoners, to proclaim the year of the Lord's favor and the day of vengeance of our God, to comfort all who mourn."

Jesus' ministry and teachings reflect the mercy and compassion prophesied by Isaiah.

Matthew 5:7 (NIV): "Blessed are the merciful, for they will be shown mercy."

Matthew 5:4 (NIV): "Blessed are those who mourn, for they will be comforted."

Jesus teaches the value of mercy and the promise of comfort for those who mourn, mirroring Isaiah's message of God's compassion and deliverance.

Peace and Reconciliation

Isaiah 9:6 (NIV): "For to us a child is born, to us a son is given, and the government will be on his shoulders. And he will be called Wonderful Counselor, Mighty God, Everlasting Father, Prince of Peace."

Isaiah 52:7 (NIV): "How beautiful on the mountains are the feet of those who bring good news, who proclaim peace, who bring good tidings, who proclaim salvation, who say to Zion, 'Your God reigns!'"

Jesus, the Prince of Peace, emphasizes peace and reconciliation in His teachings.

Matthew 5:9 (NIV): "Blessed are the peacemakers, for they will be called children of God."

Matthew 5:23-24 (NIV): "Therefore, if you are offering your gift at the altar and there remember that your brother or sister has something against you, leave your gift there in front of the altar. First go and be reconciled to them; then come and offer your gift."

Jesus calls His followers to be peacemakers and to seek reconciliation, embodying the peace prophesied in Isaiah.

Light and Salvation

Isaiah 9:2 (NIV): "The people walking in darkness have seen a great light; on those living in the land of deep darkness a light has dawned."

Isaiah 42:6-7 (NIV): "I, the Lord, have called you in righteousness; I will take hold of your hand. I will keep you and will make you to be a covenant for the people and a light for the Gentiles, to open eyes that are blind, to free captives from prison and to release from the dungeon those who sit in darkness."

Jesus proclaims Himself as the light of the world, fulfilling Isaiah's prophecy.

Matthew 5:14-16 (NIV): "You are the light of the world. A town built on a hill cannot be hidden. Neither do people light a lamp and put it under a bowl. Instead they put it on its stand, and it gives light to everyone in the house. In the same way, let your light shine before others, that they may see your good deeds and glorify your Father in heaven."

Jesus calls His followers to reflect His light and bring salvation to others, fulfilling Isaiah's vision of a great light for those in darkness.

Comprehensive Commentary

The alignment between Jesus' teachings and the prophecies of Isaiah is not coincidental but rather a fulfillment of God's divine plan. The themes of justice, righteousness, mercy, peace, and light permeate both Isaiah's prophecies and Jesus' ministry. Through the Sermon on the Mount, Jesus articulates these principles in a way that calls His followers to embody them in their daily lives.

Matthew Henry comments: "The teachings of Christ in the Sermon on the Mount are the very life and soul of the prophecies of Isaiah. They bring to light the true nature of the kingdom of God, as a kingdom of righteousness, peace, and joy in the Holy Ghost."

John Calvin, in his Institutes of the Christian Religion, writes: "The prophecies of Isaiah find their consummation in the person and work of Christ. His teachings reveal the heart of God's covenant, calling believers to live in a manner worthy of their calling, reflecting the justice, mercy, and peace that characterize the kingdom of God."

Conclusion

The teachings of Jesus in the Sermon on the Mount reflect and fulfill the principles prophesied in Isaiah. Both Isaiah and Jesus emphasize the transformative power of God's kingdom, calling believers to pursue justice, righteousness, mercy, peace, and to be a light to the world. By understanding the connection between these prophecies and Jesus' teachings, we gain a deeper appreciation of God's redemptive plan and our role in His kingdom.

As we strive to live according to the principles outlined in the Sermon on the Mount, we participate in the fulfillment of Isaiah's vision, bringing the light of Christ to a world in need of hope and salvation. This chapter highlights the profound continuity between the Old Testament prophecies and the New Testament teachings, revealing the divine coherence of God's message to humanity.

Parables of the Kingdom

Jesus frequently used parables to convey profound spiritual truths about the Kingdom of God. These parables, drawn from everyday life, are simple yet rich in meaning, providing insights into the nature of God's kingdom and the responses required from His followers. This chapter will analyze two of Jesus' most significant parables: the Parable of the Sower and the Parable of the Prodigal Son. Through expository study and comprehensive commentary supported by Strong's Concordance, we will uncover the deeper meanings and implications of these parables.

The Parable of the Sower

Matthew 13:3-9 (NIV):

"Then he told them many things in parables, saying: 'A farmer went out to sow his seed. As he was scattering the seed, some fell along the path, and the birds came and ate it up. Some fell on rocky places, where it did not have much soil. It sprang up quickly, because the soil was shallow. But when the sun came up, the plants were scorched, and they withered because they had no root. Other seed fell among thorns, which grew up and choked the plants. Still other seed fell on good soil, where it produced a crop—a hundred, sixty or thirty times what was sown. Whoever has ears, let them hear.'"

Explanation by Jesus

Matthew 13:18-23 (NIV):

"Listen then to what the parable of the sower means: When anyone hears the message about the kingdom and does not understand it, the evil one comes and snatches away what was sown in their heart. This is the seed sown along the path. The seed falling on rocky ground refers to someone who hears the word and at once receives it with joy. But since they have no root, they last only a short time. When trouble or persecution comes because of the word, they quickly fall away. The seed falling among the thorns refers to someone who hears the word, but the worries of this life and the deceitfulness of wealth choke the word, making it unfruitful. But the seed falling on good soil refers to someone who hears the word and understands it. This is the one who produces a crop, yielding a hundred, sixty or thirty times what was sown.'"

Analysis

1. The Sower: Represents Jesus or anyone who proclaims the word of God.

2. The Seed: Symbolizes the word of the kingdom (Strong's Concordance G4690, "σπέρμα" - sperma).

3. The Path: Represents those who hear the word but do not understand it. The evil one (Satan) quickly takes away what was sown (Strong's Concordance G4190, "πονηρός" - ponēros, meaning evil or wicked).

4. Rocky Places: Symbolize those who receive the word with joy but have no deep root. They fall away when trouble or persecution arises (Strong's Concordance G4073, "πέτρα" - petra, meaning rock).

5. Thorns: Represent those who hear the word but are choked by life's worries and the deceitfulness of wealth (Strong's Concordance G173, "ἀκάνθαι" - akanthai, meaning thorns).

6. Good Soil: Represents those who hear and understand the word, producing a fruitful crop (Strong's Concordance G1093, "γῆ" - gē, meaning earth or soil).

This parable illustrates the various responses to the gospel message and the factors that influence spiritual growth and fruitfulness. It highlights the importance of understanding, perseverance, and the rejection of worldly distractions to bear fruit for God's kingdom.

The Parable of the Prodigal Son

Luke 15:11-32 (NIV):

"Jesus continued: 'There was a man who had two sons. The younger one said to his father, "Father, give me my share of the estate." So he divided his property between them. Not long after that, the younger son got together all he had, set off for a distant country and there squandered his wealth in wild living. After he had spent everything, there was a severe famine in that whole country, and he began to be in need. So he went and hired himself out to a citizen of that country, who sent him to his fields to feed pigs. He longed to fill his stomach with the pods that the pigs were eating, but no one gave him anything. When he came to his senses, he said, "How many of my father's hired servants have food to spare, and here I am starving to death! I will set out and go back to my father and say to him: Father, I have sinned against heaven and against you. I am no longer worthy to be called your son; make me like one of your hired servants." So he got up and went to his father. But while he was still a long way off, his father saw him and was filled with compassion for him; he ran to his son, threw his arms around him and kissed him. The son said to him, "Father, I have sinned against heaven and against you. I am no longer worthy to be called your son." But the father said to his servants, "Quick! Bring the best robe and put it on him. Put a ring on his finger and sandals on his feet. Bring the fattened calf and kill it. Let's have a feast and celebrate. For this son of mine was dead and is alive again; he was lost and is found." So they began to celebrate. Meanwhile, the older son was in the field. When he came near the house, he heard music and dancing. So he called one of the servants and asked him what was going on. "Your brother has come," he replied, "and your father has killed the fattened calf because he has him back safe and sound." The older brother became angry and refused to go in. So his father went out and pleaded with him. But he answered his father, "Look! All these years I've been slaving for you and never disobeyed your orders. Yet you never gave me even a young goat so I could celebrate with my friends. But when this son of yours who has squandered your property with prostitutes comes home, you kill the fattened calf for him!" "My son," the father said, "you are always with me, and everything I have is yours. But we had to celebrate and be glad, because this brother of yours was dead and is alive again; he was lost and is found.""

Analysis

1. The Father: Represents God, characterized by His loving and forgiving nature (Strong's Concordance G3962, "πατήρ" - patēr, meaning father).

2. The Younger Son: Symbolizes sinners or those who turn away from God but eventually repent and return (Strong's Concordance G5207, "υἱός" - huios, meaning son).

3. The Older Son: Represents the self-righteous or those who feel they deserve more because of their perceived faithfulness (Strong's Concordance G4119, "πρεσβύτερος" - presbyteros, meaning elder or older).

4. The Inheritance: Symbolizes the blessings and resources God gives us (Strong's Concordance G3776, "οὐσία" - ousia, meaning substance or property).

5. The Far Country: Represents a place of spiritual and moral alienation from God (Strong's Concordance G5561, "χώρα" - chōra, meaning country or region).

6. The Pigs: Symbolize uncleanliness and the degradation of sin (Strong's Concordance G5519, "χοῖρος" - choiros, meaning pig).

7. The Father's Compassion: The father's running to the son and embracing him signifies God's eager and boundless mercy for repentant sinners (Strong's Concordance G4697, "σπλαγχνίζομαι" - splagchnizomai, meaning to be moved with compassion).

This parable emphasizes God's unconditional love and readiness to forgive those who repent. It contrasts the attitudes of the two sons, highlighting themes of repentance, grace, and the dangers of self-righteousness.

Comprehensive Commentary

Both parables offer deep insights into the nature of God's kingdom and the responses He seeks from His followers. The Parable of the Sower illustrates the different ways people receive and respond to the word of God, emphasizing the need for understanding, perseverance, and a rejection of worldly distractions to bear fruit. The Parable of the Prodigal Son underscores God's boundless mercy and readiness to forgive, while also warning against self-righteousness and lack of compassion.

Matthew Henry comments: "In the Parable of the Sower, we see the various hindrances to spiritual growth, but also the promise of a bountiful harvest for those who truly receive the word. In the Parable of the Prodigal Son, we witness the father's tender mercy and the joy of repentance and restoration."

John Calvin, in his Institutes of the Christian Religion, writes: "These parables reveal the heart of God and the nature of His kingdom. They call us to examine our own responses to His word and to embrace His grace with humility and gratitude."

Conclusion

The parables of Jesus are powerful tools for understanding the kingdom of God and the principles by which it operates. The Parable of the Sower and the Parable of the Prodigal Son, in particular, offer profound lessons on how we should receive God's word, respond to His grace, and live out our faith.

As we reflect on these parables, we are called to cultivate a heart that is receptive to God's word, to persevere in faith despite challenges, and to embrace the boundless mercy and forgiveness that God offers. By doing so, we participate in the life of the kingdom and bear fruit that glorifies God.

This chapter has provided an in-depth analysis of two of Jesus' most significant parables, highlighting their relevance and enduring impact on our understanding of the kingdom of God.

The Fulfillment of Isaiah's Vision of a New Covenant and Kingdom

The prophet Isaiah painted a vivid picture of a future where God's kingdom would be established in righteousness and peace. Central to Isaiah's vision is the promise of a new covenant and a reign characterized by justice, mercy, and divine presence. This chapter will explore how Jesus Christ fulfills Isaiah's vision of a new covenant and kingdom, using

Bible verses as references and providing an expository study with comprehensive commentary supported by Strong's Concordance.

Isaiah's Vision of a New Covenant

Isaiah 55:3 (NIV): "Give ear and come to me; listen, that you may live. I will make an everlasting covenant with you, my faithful love promised to David."

Isaiah 59:21 (NIV): "As for me, this is my covenant with them," says the Lord. 'My Spirit, who is on you, will not depart from you, and my words that I have put in your mouth will always be on your lips, on the lips of your children and on the lips of their descendants—from this time on and forever,' says the Lord."

Isaiah's prophecies speak of an everlasting covenant characterized by God's steadfast love and the enduring presence of His Spirit. This new covenant is not just a renewal of previous promises but a transformative relationship between God and His people.

Jesus as the Fulfillment of the New Covenant

Jeremiah, a contemporary of Isaiah, also spoke of a new covenant, providing further context for understanding its fulfillment in Jesus.

Jeremiah 31:31-34 (NIV): "The days are coming," declares the Lord, 'when I will make a new covenant with the people of Israel and with the people of Judah. It will not be like the covenant I made with their ancestors when I took them by the hand to lead them out of Egypt, because they broke my covenant, though I was a husband to them," declares the Lord. 'This is the covenant I will make with the people of Israel after that time," declares the Lord. 'I will put my law in their minds and write it on their hearts. I will be their God, and they will be my people. No longer will they teach their neighbor, or say to one another, "Know the Lord," because they will all know me, from the least of them to the greatest," declares the Lord. 'For I will forgive their wickedness and will remember their sins no more.'"

Jesus Institutes the New Covenant

Luke 22:20 (NIV): "In the same way, after the supper he took the cup, saying, 'This cup is the new covenant in my blood, which is poured out for you.'"

Hebrews 8:6-13 (NIV): "But in fact the ministry Jesus has received is as superior to theirs as the covenant of which he is mediator is superior to the old one, since the new covenant is established on better promises. For if there had been nothing wrong with that first covenant, no place would have been sought for another. But God found fault with the people and said: 'The days are coming, declares the Lord, when I will make a new covenant with the people of Israel and with the people of Judah. It will not be like the covenant I made with their ancestors when I took them by the hand to lead them out of Egypt, because they did not remain faithful to my covenant, and I turned away from them, declares the Lord. This is the covenant I will establish with the people of Israel after that time, declares the Lord. I will put my laws in their minds and write them on their hearts. I will be their God, and they will be my people. No longer will they teach their neighbor, or say to one another, "Know the Lord," because they will all know me, from the least of them to the greatest. For I will forgive their wickedness and will remember their sins no more.' By calling this covenant 'new,' he has made the first one obsolete; and what is obsolete and outdated will soon disappear."

Jesus' death and resurrection established the new covenant, fulfilling Isaiah's vision and Jeremiah's prophecy. This covenant is marked by internal transformation, forgiveness of sins, and a direct, personal relationship with God.

Isaiah's Vision of a New Kingdom

Isaiah 9:6-7 (NIV): "For to us a child is born, to us a son is given, and the government will be on his shoulders. And he will be called Wonderful Counselor, Mighty God, Everlasting Father, Prince of Peace. Of the greatness of his government and peace there will be no end. He will reign on David's throne and over his kingdom, establishing and upholding it with justice and righteousness from that time on and forever. The zeal of the Lord Almighty will accomplish this."

Isaiah 11:1-5 (NIV): "A shoot will come up from the stump of Jesse; from his roots a Branch will bear fruit. The Spirit of the Lord will rest on him—the Spirit of wisdom and of understanding, the Spirit of counsel and of might, the Spirit of the knowledge and fear of the Lord—and he will delight in the fear of the Lord. He will not judge by what he sees with his eyes, or decide by what he hears with his ears; but with righteousness he will judge the needy, with justice he will give decisions for the poor of the earth. He will strike the earth with the rod of his mouth; with the breath of his lips he will slay the wicked. Righteousness will be his belt and faithfulness the sash around his waist."

Isaiah 32:1-4 (NIV): "See, a king will reign in righteousness and rulers will rule with justice. Each one will be like a shelter from the wind and a refuge from the storm, like streams of water in the desert and the shadow of a great rock in a thirsty land. Then the eyes of those who see will no longer be closed, and the ears of those who hear will listen.

The fearful heart will know and understand, and the stammering tongue will be fluent and clear."

Jesus and the Kingdom of God

Jesus' ministry repeatedly emphasized the arrival and nature of God's kingdom, fulfilling Isaiah's prophetic vision.

Mark 1:15 (NIV): "'The time has come,' he said. 'The kingdom of God has come near. Repent and believe the good news!'"

Luke 17:20-21 (NIV): "Once, on being asked by the Pharisees when the kingdom of God would come, Jesus replied, 'The coming of the kingdom of God is not something that can be observed, nor will people say, "Here it is," or "There it is," because the kingdom of God is in your midst.'"

Characteristics of the Kingdom

1. Righteousness and Justice: As prophesied by Isaiah, Jesus' kingdom is characterized by righteousness and justice.

Matthew 5:6 (NIV): "Blessed are those who hunger and thirst for righteousness, for they will be filled."

Matthew 6:33 (NIV): "But seek first his kingdom and his righteousness, and all these things will be given to you as well."

2. Peace: Jesus is the Prince of Peace, and His kingdom brings true peace.

John 14:27 (NIV): "Peace I leave with you; my peace I give you. I do not give to you as the world gives. Do not let your hearts be troubled and do not be afraid."

3. Healing and Restoration: Isaiah's vision included healing and restoration, which Jesus fulfilled through His ministry.

Matthew 11:4-5 (NIV): "Jesus replied, 'Go back and report to John what you hear and see: The blind receive sight, the lame walk, those who have leprosy are cleansed, the deaf hear, the dead are raised, and the good news is proclaimed to the poor.'"

4. Inclusion of the Gentiles: Isaiah prophesied that the kingdom would include all nations.

Isaiah 49:6 (NIV): "He says: 'It is too small a thing for you to be my servant to restore the tribes of Jacob and bring back those of Israel I have kept. I will also make you a light for the Gentiles, that my salvation may reach to the ends of the earth.'"

Matthew 28:19-20 (NIV): "Therefore go and make disciples of all nations, baptizing them in the name of the Father and of the Son and of the Holy Spirit, and teaching them to obey everything I have commanded you. And surely I am with you always, to the very end of the age."

Comprehensive Commentary

Isaiah's prophecies about a new covenant and a righteous, peace-filled kingdom find their ultimate fulfillment in Jesus Christ. The new covenant, instituted by Jesus through His sacrificial death, brings forgiveness, transformation, and a direct relationship with God. The kingdom of God, as proclaimed and demonstrated by Jesus, embodies righteousness, justice, peace, healing, and inclusivity.

Matthew Henry comments: "In Christ, we see the fulfillment of all the promises made to the fathers. The new covenant established by His blood is the realization of God's gracious purposes, and His kingdom is the manifestation of divine righteousness and peace on earth."

John Calvin, in his Institutes of the Christian Religion, writes: "The fulfillment of Isaiah's prophecies in Christ assures us of God's faithfulness and the certainty of His promises. The new covenant is superior in every way, providing not only the remission of sins but also the renewal of our hearts by the Spirit. The kingdom of God, inaugurated by Christ, is a present reality that calls us to live under His righteous and peaceable rule."

Conclusion

Jesus Christ fulfills Isaiah's vision of a new covenant and a kingdom characterized by righteousness, peace, and divine presence. Through His life, death, and resurrection,

Jesus inaugurated the new covenant, providing forgiveness and transformation for all who believe. His proclamation and demonstration of the kingdom of God reveal the nature of His reign and the values of His kingdom.

As followers of Christ, we are called to live in the reality of this new covenant and to embody the principles of God's kingdom in our daily lives. By doing so, we participate in the fulfillment of Isaiah's vision and bear witness to the transformative power of God's love and grace.

This chapter has explored how Jesus fulfills Isaiah's vision of a new covenant and kingdom, providing a rich and comprehensive understanding of the continuity and fulfillment of God's redemptive plan as revealed in Scripture.

CHAPTER 03

JESUS' MIRACLES AND AUTHORITY – HEALING THE SICK

The Gospels record numerous instances where Jesus performed healing miracles, demonstrating His divine authority and compassion. These miracles not only provided immediate physical relief but also served as signs of the coming kingdom of God and the fulfillment of Old Testament prophecies. In this chapter, we will examine several examples of Jesus' healing miracles, focusing on curing the blind and raising the dead, to understand their significance and the deeper truths they reveal about His ministry.

Healing the Blind Man (John 9)

John 9:1-7 (NIV):

"As he went along, he saw a man blind from birth. His disciples asked him, 'Rabbi, who sinned, this man or his parents, that he was born blind?' 'Neither this man nor his parents sinned,' said Jesus, 'but this happened so that the works of God might be displayed in him. As long as it is day, we must do the works of him who sent me. Night is coming, when no one can work. While I am in the world, I am the light of the world.' After saying this, he spit on the ground, made some mud with the saliva, and put it on the man's eyes. 'Go,' he told him, 'wash in the Pool of Siloam' (this word means 'Sent'). So the man went and washed, and came home seeing."

Analysis

1. Blind from Birth: The man was born blind, which signifies a condition beyond natural remedy (Strong's Concordance G5185, "τυφλός" - typhlos, meaning blind).

2. Question of Sin: The disciples' question reflects a common belief that physical ailments were a direct result of sin. Jesus refutes this by indicating that the man's blindness was an opportunity to display God's works (Strong's Concordance G264, "ἁμαρτία" - hamartia, meaning sin).

3. Jesus as the Light of the World: Jesus' statement, "I am the light of the world," emphasizes His role in bringing spiritual illumination and physical healing (Strong's Concordance G5457, "φῶς" - phōs, meaning light).

4. The Method of Healing: Jesus uses saliva and mud, an unconventional method, showing that healing can come through various means and demonstrating His creative power (Strong's Concordance G3445, "πηλός" - pēlos, meaning mud or clay).

5. Obedience and Faith: The man's healing required obedience; he had to wash in the Pool of Siloam. This act of faith was integral to his healing (Strong's Concordance G4724, "Σιλωάμ" - Silōam, meaning Sent).

This miracle signifies Jesus' authority over physical ailments and His power to restore both physical and spiritual sight. It also illustrates that suffering can serve a greater purpose in revealing God's glory.

Raising Lazarus from the Dead (John 11)

John 11:1-44 (NIV):

"Now a man named Lazarus was sick. He was from Bethany, the village of Mary and her sister Martha. (This Mary, whose brother Lazarus now lay sick, was the same one who poured perfume on the Lord and wiped his feet with her hair.) So the sisters sent word to Jesus, 'Lord, the one you love is sick.' When he heard this, Jesus said, 'This sickness will not end in death. No, it is for God's glory so that God's Son may be glorified through it.' Now Jesus loved Martha and her sister and Lazarus. So when he heard that Lazarus was sick, he stayed where he was two more days, and then he said to his disciples, 'Let us go back to Judea.' 'But Rabbi,' they said, 'a short while ago the Jews there tried to stone you, and yet you are going back?' Jesus answered, 'Are there not twelve hours of daylight? Anyone who walks in the daytime will not stumble, for they see by this world's light. It is when a person walks at night that they stumble, for they have no light.' After he had said this, he went on to tell them, 'Our friend Lazarus has fallen asleep; but I am going there to wake him up.' His disciples replied, 'Lord, if he sleeps, he will get better.' Jesus had been speaking of his death, but his disciples thought he meant natural sleep. So then he told them plainly, 'Lazarus is dead, and for your sake I am glad I was not there, so that you may believe. But let us go to him.' Then Thomas (also known as Didymus) said to the rest of the disciples, 'Let us also go, that we may die with him.' On his arrival, Jesus found that Lazarus had already been in the tomb for four days. Now Bethany was less than two miles from Jerusalem, and many Jews had come to Martha and Mary to comfort them in the loss of their brother. When Martha heard that Jesus was coming, she went out to meet him, but Mary stayed at home. 'Lord,' Martha said to Jesus, 'if you had been here, my brother would not have died. But I know that even now God will give you whatever you ask.' Jesus said to her, 'Your brother will rise again.' Martha answered, 'I know he will rise again in the resurrection at the last day.' Jesus said to her, 'I am the resurrection and the life. The one who believes in me will live, even though they die; and whoever lives by believing in me will never die. Do you believe this?' 'Yes, Lord,' she replied, 'I believe that you are the Messiah, the Son of God, who is to come into the world.' After she had said this, she went back and called her sister Mary aside. 'The Teacher is here,' she said, 'and is asking for you.' When Mary heard this, she got up quickly and went to him. Now Jesus had not yet entered the village, but was still at the place where Martha had met him. When the Jews who had been with Mary in the house, comforting her, noticed how quickly she got up and went out, they followed her, supposing she was going to the tomb to mourn there. When Mary reached the place where Jesus was and saw him, she fell at his feet and said, 'Lord, if you had been here, my brother would not have died.' When Jesus saw her weeping, and the Jews who had come along with her also weeping, he was deeply moved in spirit and troubled. 'Where have you laid him?' he asked. 'Come and see, Lord,' they replied. Jesus wept. Then the Jews said, 'See how he loved him!' But some of them said, 'Could not he who opened the eyes of the blind man have kept this man from dying?' Jesus, once more deeply moved, came to the tomb. It was a cave with a stone laid across the entrance. 'Take away the stone,' he said. 'But, Lord,' said Martha, the sister of the dead man, 'by this time there is a bad odor, for he has been there four days.' Then Jesus said, 'Did I not tell you that if you believe, you will see the glory of God?' So they took away the stone. Then Jesus looked up and said, 'Father, I thank you that you have heard me. I knew that you always hear me, but I said this for the benefit of the people standing here, that they may believe that you sent me.' When he had said this, Jesus called in a loud voice, 'Lazarus, come out!' The dead man came out, his hands and feet wrapped with strips of linen, and a cloth around his face. Jesus said to them, 'Take off the grave clothes and let him go.'"

Analysis

1. Lazarus' Sickness and Death: Lazarus' illness and subsequent death were meant to glorify God and demonstrate Jesus' power over death (Strong's Concordance G599, "ἀποθνῄσκω" - apothnēskō, meaning to die).

2. Jesus' Delay: Jesus intentionally delays His visit, allowing Lazarus to die to show His disciples and others a greater miracle – raising the dead (Strong's Concordance G3306, "μένω" - menō, meaning to remain or stay).

3. Jesus' Compassion: Jesus weeps, showing His deep compassion and empathy for human suffering (Strong's Concordance G1145, "δακρύω" - dakryō, meaning to weep).

4. Declaration of Authority: Jesus declares, "I am the resurrection and the life," affirming His divine authority over life and death (Strong's Concordance G386, "ἀνάστασις" - anastasis, meaning resurrection).

5. Raising Lazarus: The miracle of raising Lazarus demonstrates Jesus' power over death and foreshadows His own resurrection (Strong's Concordance G2523, "φωνέω" - phōneō, meaning to call out).

This miracle highlights Jesus' authority over life and death, serving as a powerful testimony to His divine nature and the promise of eternal life for believers.

Healing a Paralytic (Mark 2:1-12)

Mark 2:1-12 (NIV):

"A few days later, when Jesus again entered Capernaum, the people heard that he had come home. They gathered in such large numbers that there was no room left, not even outside the door, and he preached the word to them. Some men came, bringing to him a paralyzed man, carried by four of them. Since they could not get him to Jesus because of the crowd, they made an opening in the roof above Jesus by digging through it and then lowered the mat the man was lying on. When Jesus saw their faith, he said to the paralyzed man, 'Son, your sins are forgiven.' Now some teachers of the law were sitting there, thinking to themselves, 'Why does this fellow talk like that? He's blaspheming! Who can forgive sins but God alone?' Immediately Jesus knew in his spirit that this was what they were thinking in their hearts, and he said to them, 'Why are you thinking these things? Which is easier: to say to this paralyzed man, "Your sins are forgiven," or to say, "Get up, take your mat and walk"? But I want you to know that the Son of Man has authority on earth to forgive sins.' So he said to the man, 'I tell you, get up, take your mat and go home.' He got up, took his mat and walked out in full view of them all. This amazed everyone and they praised God, saying, 'We have never seen anything like this!'"

Analysis

1. Paralysis: The man's paralysis symbolizes a condition of helplessness and dependency (Strong's Concordance G3886, "παραλυτικός" - paralytikos, meaning paralytic).

2. Faith: The faith of the paralyzed man's friends is highlighted as they go to great lengths to bring him to Jesus (Strong's Concordance G4102, "πίστις" - pistis, meaning faith).

3. Forgiveness of Sins: Jesus' declaration of forgiveness emphasizes His authority to forgive sins, which was perceived as blasphemy by the religious leaders (Strong's Concordance G863, "ἀφίημι" - aphiēmi, meaning to forgive or send away).

4. Healing as a Sign: The physical healing serves as a visible sign of the man's spiritual restoration and Jesus' authority (Strong's Concordance G2390, "ἰάομαι" - iaomai, meaning to heal).

This miracle underscores Jesus' authority to forgive sins and heal physical ailments, demonstrating that He has the power to address both spiritual and physical needs.

Healing the Woman with the Issue of Blood (Mark 5:25-34)

Mark 5:25-34 (NIV):

"And a woman was there who had been subject to bleeding for twelve years. She had suffered a great deal under the care of many doctors and had spent all she had, yet instead of getting better she grew worse. When she heard about Jesus, she came up behind him in the crowd and touched his cloak, because she thought, 'If I just touch his clothes, I will be healed.' Immediately her bleeding stopped and she felt in her body that she was freed from her suffering. At once Jesus realized that power had gone out from him. He turned around in the crowd and asked, 'Who touched my clothes?' 'You see the people crowding against you,' his disciples answered, 'and yet you can ask, "Who touched me?"' But Jesus kept looking around to see who had done it. Then the woman, knowing what had happened to her, came and fell at his feet and, trembling with fear, told him the whole truth. He said to her, 'Daughter, your faith has healed you. Go in peace and be freed from your suffering.'"

Analysis

1. Chronic Illness: The woman's long-term suffering and unsuccessful treatments highlight her desperate condition (Strong's Concordance G4512, "ῥύσις" - rhysis, meaning a flow or issue of blood).

2. Faith and Healing: Her belief that touching Jesus' cloak would heal her demonstrates strong faith (Strong's Concordance G2983, "λαμβάνω" - lambanō, meaning to take or receive).

3. Immediate Healing: The instant cessation of her bleeding signifies the power of Jesus' healing touch (Strong's Concordance G2390, "ἰάομαι" - iaomai, meaning to heal).

4. Jesus' Awareness: Jesus' recognition that power had gone out from Him shows His divine sensitivity and the personal nature of His healing (Strong's Concordance G1411, "δύναμις" - dynamis, meaning power or strength).

5. Public Affirmation: Jesus publicly acknowledges the woman's faith and healing, restoring her dignity and social standing (Strong's Concordance G1510, "εἰμί" - eimi, meaning to be or exist).

This miracle emphasizes the personal nature of Jesus' healing power and the importance of faith in receiving divine intervention.

Comprehensive Commentary

The healing miracles of Jesus provide profound insights into His divine authority and compassionate nature. Each miracle not only addresses physical ailments but also reveals deeper spiritual truths about faith, forgiveness, and the kingdom of God. Through these acts, Jesus fulfills the messianic prophecies of the Old Testament, demonstrating that He is the promised Savior who brings wholeness and restoration.

Matthew Henry comments: "In every miracle, we see the hand of God working through Christ to demonstrate His power, compassion, and authority. These acts of healing are signs of the greater spiritual healing and restoration that Christ offers to all who believe."

John Calvin, in his Institutes of the Christian Religion, writes: "The miracles of Christ are not merely demonstrations of power but are meant to point us to the deeper reality of

His divine mission. They assure us of His ability to save and restore us, both physically and spiritually."

Conclusion

Jesus' healing miracles are powerful testimonies to His divine authority and compassion. Through curing the blind, raising the dead, and healing various ailments, Jesus not only alleviated physical suffering but also revealed the nature of God's kingdom and His redemptive mission. These miracles invite us to have faith in Jesus, recognizing Him as the source of both physical and spiritual healing.

As we reflect on these miracles, we are called to trust in Jesus' power and compassion, seeking His healing touch in our own lives and extending His love and grace to others. This chapter has provided an in-depth analysis of some of Jesus' most significant healing miracles, highlighting their significance and enduring impact on our understanding of His ministry.

Healing the Sick – Isaiah's Prophecies of a Healer and Restorer

The prophet Isaiah foretold the coming of a Messiah who would heal and restore the people of God. His prophecies provide a vivid picture of the physical and spiritual healing that the Messiah would bring. This chapter will explore Isaiah's prophecies of a healer and restorer, particularly focusing on Isaiah 35:5-6, and how these prophecies are fulfilled in the ministry of Jesus Christ. Through expository study and comprehensive commentary supported by Strong's Concordance, we will uncover the profound significance of these prophetic declarations.

Isaiah's Prophecies of a Healer and Restorer

Isaiah 35:5-6 (NIV): "Then will the eyes of the blind be opened and the ears of the deaf unstopped. Then will the lame leap like a deer, and the mute tongue shout for joy. Water will gush forth in the wilderness and streams in the desert."

These verses are part of a broader prophecy describing the transformation and restoration that will occur when God's kingdom is fully realized. Isaiah's vision includes the healing of physical ailments, symbolizing the renewal and restoration of all creation under God's reign.

Analysis

1. Eyes of the Blind Opened: The opening of the blind's eyes signifies the restoration of sight, both physically and spiritually (Strong's Concordance H5787, "עִוֵּר" - ʿiwer, meaning blind).

2. Ears of the Deaf Unstopped: This signifies the restoration of hearing, symbolizing the ability to hear and understand God's word (Strong's Concordance H2795, "חֵרֵשׁ" - cheresh, meaning deaf).

3. The Lame Leaping: This symbolizes the restoration of mobility and strength, representing the renewal of physical bodies and the joy of salvation (Strong's Concordance H6455, "פִּסֵּחַ" - pisēach, meaning lame).

4. Mute Tongue Shouting for Joy: This signifies the restoration of speech, representing the joy and praise that come from being healed and restored by God (Strong's Concordance H483, "אִלֵּם" - ʾillēm, meaning mute).

5. Water in the Wilderness: This symbolizes life and renewal in barren places, representing the transformative power of God's presence (Strong's Concordance H4057, "מִדְבָּר" - midbar, meaning wilderness).

Fulfillment in Jesus' Ministry

Isaiah's prophecies find their fulfillment in the ministry of Jesus, who performed numerous healing miracles that directly correspond to the ailments mentioned in Isaiah 35:5-6.

Healing the Blind

John 9:1-7 (NIV):

"As he went along, he saw a man blind from birth. His disciples asked him, 'Rabbi, who sinned, this man or his parents, that he was born blind?' 'Neither this man nor his parents sinned,' said Jesus, 'but this happened so that the works of God might be displayed in him. As long as it is day, we must do the works of him who sent me. Night is coming, when no one can work. While I am in the world, I am the light of the world.' After saying this, he spit on the ground, made some mud with the saliva, and put it on the man's eyes. 'Go,' he told him, 'wash in the Pool of Siloam' (this word means 'Sent'). So the man went and washed, and came home seeing."

Analysis

1. Restoration of Sight: The miracle of giving sight to a man blind from birth demonstrates Jesus' divine power and fulfills Isaiah's prophecy of opening the eyes of the blind (Strong's Concordance G5185, "τυφλός" - typhlos, meaning blind).

2. Jesus as the Light: Jesus' declaration, "I am the light of the world," signifies His role in bringing spiritual illumination and physical healing (Strong's Concordance G5457, "φῶς" - phōs, meaning light).

This miracle is a direct fulfillment of Isaiah's prophecy, showcasing Jesus as the promised healer who brings light and restoration.

Healing the Deaf and Mute

Mark 7:31-37 (NIV):

"Then Jesus left the vicinity of Tyre and went through Sidon, down to the Sea of Galilee and into the region of the Decapolis. There some people brought to him a man who was deaf and could hardly talk, and they begged Jesus to place his hand on him. After he took him aside, away from the crowd, Jesus put his fingers into the man's ears. Then he spit and touched the man's tongue. He looked up to heaven and with a deep sigh said to him, 'Ephphatha!' (which means 'Be opened!'). At this, the man's ears were opened, his tongue was loosened and he began to speak plainly. Jesus commanded them not to tell anyone. But the more he did so, the more they kept talking about it. People were overwhelmed with amazement. 'He has done everything well,' they said. 'He even makes the deaf hear and the mute speak.'"

Analysis

1. Healing of Deafness: Jesus' healing of the man's deafness fulfills Isaiah's prophecy of unstopping the ears of the deaf (Strong's Concordance G2974, "κωφός" - kōphos, meaning deaf).

2. Healing of Mutism: The loosening of the man's tongue and his ability to speak plainly fulfill the prophecy of the mute tongue shouting for joy (Strong's Concordance G2164, "μογγιλάλος" - mogilalos, meaning mute).

3. Command and Compassion: Jesus' command, "Ephphatha," and His compassionate touch highlight His authority and care in healing (Strong's Concordance G455, "διανοίγω" - dianoigō, meaning to open fully).

This miracle exemplifies Jesus' fulfillment of Isaiah's vision of healing and restoration, as He brings both physical and spiritual wholeness.

Healing the Lame

John 5:1-9 (NIV):

"Some time later, Jesus went up to Jerusalem for one of the Jewish festivals. Now there is in Jerusalem near the Sheep Gate a pool, which in Aramaic is called Bethesda and which is surrounded by five covered colonnades. Here a great number of disabled people used to lie—the blind, the lame, the paralyzed. One who was there had been an invalid for thirty-eight years. When Jesus saw him lying there and learned that he had been in this condition for a long time, he asked him, 'Do you want to get well?' 'Sir,' the invalid replied, 'I have no one to help me into the pool when the water is stirred. While I am trying to get in, someone else goes down ahead of me.' Then Jesus said to him, 'Get up! Pick up your mat and walk.' At once the man was cured; he picked up his mat and walked. The day on which this took place was a Sabbath."

Analysis

1. Restoration of Mobility: The healing of the lame man at Bethesda fulfills Isaiah's prophecy of the lame leaping like a deer (Strong's Concordance G5560, "χωλὸς" - chōlos, meaning lame).

2. Immediate Healing: The instantaneous nature of the healing demonstrates Jesus' divine power and authority (Strong's Concordance G2388, "ἰσχύω" - ischyō, meaning to be strong or able).

3. Jesus' Command: Jesus' command, "Get up! Pick up your mat and walk," emphasizes His authority and the transformative power of His word (Strong's Concordance G1453, "ἐγείρω" - egeirō, meaning to raise up or awaken).

This miracle underscores Jesus' ability to restore physical capabilities, aligning with Isaiah's prophecy of physical and spiritual renewal.

Comprehensive Commentary

Isaiah's prophecies of a healer and restorer are vividly fulfilled in the ministry of Jesus Christ. His miracles of healing the blind, deaf, mute, and lame illustrate the comprehensive nature of His restorative work. These acts of healing serve as signs of the kingdom of God, where wholeness and restoration are central themes.

Matthew Henry comments: "In Christ, we see the fulfillment of Isaiah's vision of a healer who brings not only physical restoration but also spiritual renewal. Each miracle points to the greater reality of the kingdom of God and the transformative power of the Messiah."

John Calvin, in his Institutes of the Christian Religion, writes: "The healing miracles of Christ demonstrate His divine authority and the fulfillment of the prophetic promises. They reveal the nature of His mission and the comprehensive scope of His salvation, which encompasses both body and soul."

Conclusion

Isaiah's prophecies of a healer and restorer find their ultimate fulfillment in Jesus Christ. Through His miracles, Jesus demonstrates His divine authority and compassion, bringing physical and spiritual healing to those in need. These acts of healing not only address immediate ailments but also point to the broader reality of God's kingdom, where restoration and renewal are paramount.

As we reflect on these miracles, we are reminded of Jesus' power to heal and restore us in every aspect of our lives. This chapter has explored Isaiah's prophetic vision and its fulfillment in Jesus' ministry, providing a deeper understanding of the continuity and fulfillment of God's redemptive plan as revealed in Scripture.

Power Over Nature

The miracles of Jesus extend beyond healing the sick to demonstrating His authority over the natural world. Two of the most striking examples are His calming of the storm and His walking on water. These miracles not only reveal

Jesus' divine power but also serve as profound lessons on faith and trust in Him. In this chapter, we will explore these miracles in detail, analyzing their significance and the deeper truths they convey about Jesus' nature and mission.

Calming the Storm

Mark 4:35-41 (NIV):

"That day when evening came, he said to his disciples, 'Let us go over to the other side.' Leaving the crowd behind, they took him along, just as he was, in the boat. There were also other boats with him. A furious squall came up, and the waves broke over the boat, so that it was nearly swamped. Jesus was in the stern, sleeping on a cushion. The disciples woke him and said to him, 'Teacher, don't you care if we drown?' He got up, rebuked the wind and said to the waves, 'Quiet! Be still!' Then the wind died down and it was completely calm. He said to his disciples, 'Why are you so afraid? Do you still have no faith?' They were terrified and asked each other, 'Who is this? Even the wind and the waves obey him!'"

Analysis

1. Furious Squall: The sudden and violent storm signifies chaos and danger (Strong's Concordance G2978, "λαιλαψ" - lailaps, meaning whirlwind or tempest).

2. Jesus Sleeping: Jesus' calm demeanor, even while sleeping during the storm, highlights His trust in God's providence and His control over the situation (Strong's Concordance G2518, "καθεύδω" - katheudō, meaning to sleep).

3. Disciples' Fear: The disciples' panic and fear contrast sharply with Jesus' calmness, revealing their lack of faith (Strong's Concordance G1169, "δειλός" - deilos, meaning fearful or cowardly).

4. Rebuking the Wind and Waves: Jesus' command, "Quiet! Be still!" demonstrates His authority over nature, as even the elements obey Him (Strong's Concordance G2008, "ἐπιτιμάω" - epitimaō, meaning to rebuke or censure).

5. Lesson on Faith: Jesus' question to the disciples, "Why are you so afraid? Do you still have no faith?" underscores the importance of trusting in Him amidst life's storms (Strong's Concordance G4102, "πίστις" - pistis, meaning faith).

This miracle illustrates Jesus' divine power over creation and His ability to bring peace in the midst of chaos. It also teaches a vital lesson on the necessity of faith in Jesus, even when circumstances appear overwhelming.

Walking on Water

Matthew 14:22-33 (NIV):

"Immediately Jesus made the disciples get into the boat and go on ahead of him to the other side, while he dismissed the crowd. After he had dismissed them, he went up on a mountainside by himself to pray. Later that night, he was there alone, and the boat was already a considerable distance from land, buffeted by the waves because the wind was against it. Shortly before dawn Jesus went out to them, walking on the lake. When the disciples saw him walking on the lake, they were terrified. 'It's a ghost,' they said, and cried out in fear. But Jesus immediately said to them: 'Take courage! It is I. Don't be afraid.' 'Lord, if it's you,' Peter replied, 'tell me to come to you on the water.' 'Come,' he said. Then Peter got down out of the boat, walked on the water and came toward Jesus. But when he saw the wind, he was afraid and, beginning to sink, cried out, 'Lord, save me!' Immediately Jesus reached out his hand and caught him. 'You of little faith,' he said, 'why did you doubt?' And when they climbed into the boat, the wind died down. Then those who were in the boat worshiped him, saying, 'Truly you are the Son of God.'"

Analysis

1. Buffeted by Waves: The disciples' struggle against the waves symbolizes the trials and challenges of life (Strong's Concordance G928, "βασανίζω" - basanizō, meaning to torment or harass).

2. Jesus Walking on Water: Jesus' act of walking on the water demonstrates His mastery over the natural elements, a clear sign of His divine nature (Strong's Concordance G4043, "περιπατέω" - peripateō, meaning to walk).

3. Disciples' Fear and Recognition: The disciples' initial fear and subsequent recognition of Jesus highlight the revelation of His identity as the Son of God (Strong's Concordance G5326, "φάντασμα" - phantasma, meaning apparition or ghost).

4. Peter's Attempt and Failure: Peter's initial success in walking on water, followed by his fear and sinking, illustrates the mixture of faith and doubt that characterizes human responses to divine power (Strong's Concordance G3640, "ὀλιγόπιστος" - oligopistos, meaning of little faith).

5. Jesus' Rescue: Jesus' immediate response to Peter's cry for help underscores His readiness to save and support those who call upon Him in faith (Strong's Concordance G1299, "διασώζω" - diasōzō, meaning to save thoroughly).

6. Calming the Wind: The cessation of the wind upon Jesus entering the boat further emphasizes His authority over nature and His role as the bringer of peace (Strong's Concordance G3973, "παύω" - pauō, meaning to cease or stop).

This miracle reveals Jesus' power over natural laws and His ability to transcend physical limitations. It also serves as a profound lesson on faith, courage, and the importance of focusing on Jesus amidst life's storms.

Comprehensive Commentary

The miracles of calming the storm and walking on water showcase Jesus' divine authority and mastery over nature. These events are not mere demonstrations of power but serve as powerful lessons on faith, trust, and the nature of Jesus' identity as the Son of God.

Matthew Henry comments: "In these miracles, we see Christ's authority over the creation He made. The winds and waves recognize their Creator and obey His command. These acts of power remind us that in every storm of life, Christ is sovereign and present."

John Calvin, in his Institutes of the Christian Religion, writes: "The miracles of Christ over nature reveal His divinity and His lordship over all creation. They call us to trust in His sovereign power and to recognize Him as the true God who controls all things by His word."

Theological Significance

1. Revelation of Jesus' Divinity: These miracles affirm Jesus' divine nature, demonstrating that He possesses

authority over the natural world, an attribute that belongs only to God.

2. Encouragement of Faith: Both miracles emphasize the importance of faith in Jesus. The disciples' fear and doubt contrast with Jesus' calm authority, teaching believers to trust Him even in the most challenging circumstances.

3. Symbolism of Salvation: The calming of the storm and the rescue of Peter symbolize Jesus' power to save and deliver from both physical and spiritual perils. These miracles foreshadow the ultimate salvation Jesus provides through His death and resurrection.

4. Manifestation of the Kingdom of God: These miracles are signs of the kingdom of God, where Jesus' reign brings order, peace, and restoration to all creation. They point to the eschatological hope of a restored creation under Christ's rule.

Conclusion

The miracles of calming the storm and walking on water are profound demonstrations of Jesus' power over nature and His divine authority. They reveal His identity as the Son of God and teach vital lessons on faith, trust, and reliance on His saving power. Through these miracles, Jesus not only alleviated immediate physical dangers but also pointed to the deeper spiritual truths of His mission and the nature of God's kingdom.

As we reflect on these miracles, we are called to deepen our faith in Jesus, recognizing His sovereign power and trusting Him in all circumstances. This chapter has explored these significant miracles, providing a comprehensive understanding of their theological implications and enduring relevance for believers today.

Demonstration of Jesus' Divine Authority Over Creation

Jesus' miracles serve not only as acts of compassion and power but also as clear demonstrations of His divine authority over all creation. The Gospels record numerous instances where Jesus exercises control over the natural world, illustrating His divine nature and reinforcing His identity as the Son of God. This chapter will focus on two significant miracles: calming the storm and walking on water. Through these acts, Jesus reveals His sovereignty over creation, providing profound lessons on faith and trust in His divine power.

Calming the Storm

Mark 4:35-41 (NIV):

"That day when evening came, he said to his disciples, 'Let us go over to the other side.' Leaving the crowd behind, they took him along, just as he was, in the boat. There were also other boats with him. A furious squall came up, and the waves broke over the boat, so that it was nearly swamped. Jesus was in the stern, sleeping on a cushion. The disciples woke him and said to him, 'Teacher, don't you care if we drown?' He got up, rebuked the wind and said to the waves, 'Quiet! Be still!' Then the wind died down and it was completely calm. He said to his disciples, 'Why are you so afraid? Do you still have no faith?' They were terrified and asked each other, 'Who is this? Even the wind and the waves obey him!'"

Analysis

1. Furious Squall: The sudden and violent storm represents chaos and danger (Strong's Concordance G2978, "λαιλαψ" - lailaps, meaning whirlwind or tempest).

2. Jesus Sleeping: Jesus' calm demeanor while sleeping during the storm highlights His trust in God's providence and His control over the situation (Strong's Concordance G2518, "καθευδω" - katheudō, meaning to sleep).

3. Disciples' Fear: The disciples' panic and fear contrast sharply with Jesus' calmness, revealing their lack of faith (Strong's Concordance G1169, "δειλός" - deilos, meaning fearful or cowardly).

4. Rebuking the Wind and Waves: Jesus' command, "Quiet! Be still!" demonstrates His authority over nature, as even the elements obey Him (Strong's Concordance G2008, "ἐπιτιμάω" - epitimaō, meaning to rebuke or censure).

5. Lesson on Faith: Jesus' question to the disciples, "Why are you so afraid? Do you still have no faith?" underscores the importance of trusting in Him amidst life's storms (Strong's Concordance G4102, "πίστις" - pistis, meaning faith).

This miracle illustrates Jesus' divine power over creation and His ability to bring peace in the midst of chaos. It also teaches a vital lesson on the necessity of faith in Jesus, even when circumstances appear overwhelming.

Walking on Water

Matthew 14:22-33 (NIV):

"Immediately Jesus made the disciples get into the boat and go on ahead of him to the other side, while he dismissed the crowd. After he had dismissed them, he went up on a mountainside by himself to pray. Later that night, he was there alone, and the boat was already a considerable distance from land, buffeted by the waves because the wind was against it. Shortly before dawn Jesus went out to them, walking on the lake. When the disciples saw him walking on the lake, they were terrified. 'It's a ghost,' they said, and cried out in fear. But Jesus immediately said to them: 'Take courage! It is I. Don't be afraid.' 'Lord, if it's you,' Peter replied, 'tell me to come to you on the water.' 'Come,' he said. Then Peter got down out of the boat, walked on the water and came toward Jesus. But when he saw the wind, he was afraid and, beginning to sink, cried out, 'Lord, save me!' Immediately Jesus reached out his hand and caught him. 'You of little faith,' he said, 'why did you doubt?' And when they climbed into the boat, the wind died down. Then those who were in the boat worshiped him, saying, 'Truly you are the Son of God.'"

Analysis

1. Buffeted by Waves: The disciples' struggle against the waves symbolizes the trials and challenges of life (Strong's Concordance G928, "βασανίζω" - basanizō, meaning to torment or harass).

2. Jesus Walking on Water: Jesus' act of walking on the water demonstrates His mastery over the natural elements, a clear sign of His divine nature (Strong's Concordance G4043, "περιπατέω" - peripateō, meaning to walk).

3. Disciples' Fear and Recognition: The disciples' initial fear and subsequent recognition of Jesus highlight the revelation of His identity as the Son of God (Strong's Concordance G5326, "φάντασμα" - phantasma, meaning apparition or ghost).

4. Peter's Attempt and Failure: Peter's initial success in walking on water, followed by his fear and sinking, illustrates the mixture of faith and doubt that characterizes human responses to divine power (Strong's Concordance G3640, "ὀλιγόπιστος" - oligopistos, meaning of little faith).

5. Jesus' Rescue: Jesus' immediate response to Peter's cry for help underscores His readiness to save and support those who call upon Him in faith (Strong's Concordance G1299, "διασώζω" - diasōzō, meaning to save thoroughly).

6. Calming the Wind: The cessation of the wind upon Jesus entering the boat further emphasizes His authority over nature and His role as the bringer of peace (Strong's Concordance G3973, "παύω" - pauō, meaning to cease or stop).

This miracle reveals Jesus' power over natural laws and His ability to transcend physical limitations. It also serves as a profound lesson on faith, courage, and the importance of focusing on Jesus amidst life's storms.

Jesus and the Old Testament Prophecies

The miracles of Jesus not only demonstrate His authority but also fulfill Old Testament prophecies about the Messiah's dominion over creation.

Psalm 89:9 (NIV): "You rule over the surging sea; when its waves mount up, you still them."

Psalm 107:29 (NIV): "He stilled the storm to a whisper; the waves of the sea were hushed."

These Psalms, which speak of God's power over nature, find their fulfillment in Jesus' miracles. By calming the storm and walking on water, Jesus shows that He possesses the divine authority attributed to God in the Hebrew Scriptures.

Comprehensive Commentary

The miracles of calming the storm and walking on water showcase Jesus' divine authority and mastery over nature. These events are not mere demonstrations of power but serve as powerful lessons on faith, trust, and the nature of Jesus' identity as the Son of God.

Matthew Henry comments: "In these miracles, we see Christ's authority over the creation He made. The winds and waves recognize their Creator and obey His command. These acts of power remind us that in every storm of life, Christ is sovereign and present."

John Calvin, in his Institutes of the Christian Religion, writes: "The miracles of Christ over nature reveal His divinity and His lordship over all creation. They call us to trust in His sovereign power and to recognize Him as the true God who controls all things by His word."

Theological Significance

1. Revelation of Jesus' Divinity: These miracles affirm Jesus' divine nature, demonstrating that He possesses authority over the natural world, an attribute that belongs only to God.

2. Encouragement of Faith: Both miracles emphasize the importance of faith in Jesus. The disciples' fear and doubt contrast with Jesus' calm authority, teaching believers to trust Him even in the most challenging circumstances.

3. Symbolism of Salvation: The calming of the storm and the rescue of Peter symbolize Jesus' power to save and deliver from both physical and spiritual perils. These miracles foreshadow the ultimate salvation Jesus provides through His death and resurrection.

4. Manifestation of the Kingdom of God: These miracles are signs of the kingdom of God, where Jesus' reign brings order, peace, and restoration to all creation. They point to the eschatological hope of a restored creation under Christ's rule.

Conclusion

The miracles of calming the storm and walking on water are profound demonstrations of Jesus' power over nature and His divine authority. They reveal His identity as the Son of God and teach vital lessons on faith, trust, and reliance on His saving power. Through these miracles, Jesus not only alleviated immediate physical dangers but also pointed to the deeper spiritual truths of His mission and the nature of God's kingdom.

As we reflect on these miracles, we are called to deepen our faith in Jesus, recognizing His sovereign power and trusting Him in all circumstances. This chapter has explored these significant miracles, providing a comprehensive understanding of their theological implications and enduring relevance for believers today.

CHAPTER 04

THE SACRIFICIAL LAMB – THE SUFFERING SERVANT

The prophet Isaiah, in a passage often referred to as the "Suffering Servant," provides one of the most detailed and poignant prophecies about the Messiah's suffering and sacrifice. Isaiah 53 is a cornerstone of messianic prophecy, vividly portraying the pain, rejection, and ultimate purpose of the Servant's suffering. This chapter will delve into Isaiah 53, examining its prophetic details and how they are fulfilled in the life and sacrifice of Jesus Christ. Through an expository study and comprehensive commentary supported by Strong's Concordance, we will uncover the profound significance of this prophecy.

The Suffering Servant in Isaiah 53

Isaiah 53 (NIV):

1. Who has believed our message and to whom has the arm of the Lord been revealed?

- This opening question highlights the surprising and often unbelieved nature of the Servant's mission. The "arm of the Lord" signifies God's power and intervention (Strong's Concordance H2220, "זְרוֹעַ" - zĕrowa`, meaning arm or power).

2. He grew up before him like a tender shoot, and like a root out of dry ground. He had no beauty or majesty to attract us to him, nothing in his appearance that we should desire him.

- The Servant's humble beginnings and ordinary appearance emphasize His identification with humanity. The "tender shoot" and "root out of dry ground" symbolize vulnerability and unexpected emergence (Strong's Concordance H3126, "יוֹנֵק" - yonek, meaning a tender plant).

3. He was despised and rejected by mankind, a man of suffering, and familiar with pain. Like one from whom people hide their faces he was despised, and we held him in low esteem.

- The Servant's rejection and suffering are central to this prophecy. His experience of pain and rejection underscores His role in bearing humanity's burdens (Strong's Concordance H2534, "חֵמָה" - chemah, meaning wrath or indignation).

4. Surely he took up our pain and bore our suffering, yet we considered him punished by God, stricken by him, and afflicted.

- The Servant's vicarious suffering highlights His role in taking on the pain and punishment meant for others. This verse underscores the substitutionary nature of His sacrifice (Strong's Concordance H6031, "עָנָה" - anah, meaning to afflict or humble).

5. But he was pierced for our transgressions, he was crushed for our iniquities; the punishment that brought us peace was on him, and by his wounds we are healed.

- This verse explicitly states the purpose of the Servant's suffering: to atone for humanity's sins. The terms "pierced" and "crushed" indicate the severity of His sacrifice (Strong's Concordance H2490, "חָלַל" - chalal, meaning to pierce or wound).

6. We all, like sheep, have gone astray, each of us has turned to our own way; and the Lord has laid on him the iniquity of us all.

- Humanity's collective waywardness and sin are contrasted with the Servant's role in bearing these iniquities.

This verse emphasizes the comprehensive scope of His atonement (Strong's Concordance H5771, "עָוֹן" - avon, meaning iniquity or guilt).

7. He was oppressed and afflicted, yet he did not open his mouth; he was led like a lamb to the slaughter, and as a sheep before its shearers is silent, so he did not open his mouth.

- The Servant's silent acceptance of suffering highlights His meekness and submission. The imagery of a lamb led to slaughter underscores His role as a sacrificial offering (Strong's Concordance H3533, "כָּבַשׁ" - kabash, meaning to subdue or silence).

8. By oppression and judgment he was taken away. Yet who of his generation protested? For he was cut off from the land of the living; for the transgression of my people he was punished.

- The unjust treatment and death of the Servant are depicted here, showing His suffering as a result of bearing the sins of others (Strong's Concordance H1504, "גָּזַר" - gazar, meaning to cut off or divide).

9. He was assigned a grave with the wicked, and with the rich in his death, though he had done no violence, nor was any deceit in his mouth.

- Despite His innocence, the Servant's death is associated with both the wicked and the wealthy, highlighting the paradox of His burial (Strong's Concordance H7563, "רָשָׁע" - rasha`, meaning wicked or guilty).

10. Yet it was the Lord's will to crush him and cause him to suffer, and though the Lord makes his life an offering for sin, he will see his offspring and prolong his days, and the will of the Lord will prosper in his hand.

- The Servant's suffering is depicted as part of God's redemptive plan, with the promise of future vindication and prosperity (Strong's Concordance H6213, "עָשָׂה" - asah, meaning to do or make).

11. After he has suffered, he will see the light of life and be satisfied; by his knowledge my righteous servant will justify many, and he will bear their iniquities.

- The prophecy concludes with the Servant's vindication and the justification of many through His knowledge and sacrifice (Strong's Concordance H6663, "צָדַק" - tsadaq, meaning to be righteous or just).

12. Therefore I will give him a portion among the great, and he will divide the spoils with the strong, because he poured out his life unto death, and was numbered with the transgressors. For he bore the sin of many, and made intercession for the transgressors.

- The Servant's ultimate reward and exaltation are depicted, affirming the significance of His sacrificial death and intercessory role (Strong's Concordance H7725, "שׁוּב" - shuwb, meaning to return or restore).

Fulfillment in Jesus' Life and Sacrifice

The detailed prophecy in Isaiah 53 finds its fulfillment in the life, death, and resurrection of Jesus Christ. The New Testament writers repeatedly reference this chapter to illustrate how Jesus embodied the Suffering Servant.

Jesus' Suffering and Rejection

Matthew 26:67-68 (NIV): "Then they spit in his face and struck him with their fists. Others slapped him and said, 'Prophesy to us, Messiah. Who hit you?'"

John 1:11 (NIV): "He came to that which was his own, but his own did not receive him."

These verses reflect the rejection and suffering Jesus endured, fulfilling Isaiah's prophecy of the despised and rejected Servant.

Jesus' Silence Before His Accusers

Matthew 27:12-14 (NIV): "When he was accused by the chief priests and the elders, he gave no answer. Then Pilate asked him, 'Don't you hear the testimony they are bringing against you?' But Jesus made no reply, not even to a single charge—to the great amazement of the governor."

This fulfillment echoes Isaiah 53:7, where the Servant is described as being silent before His oppressors.

Jesus' Atoning Death

1 Peter 2:24 (NIV): "He himself bore our sins in his body on the cross, so that we might die to sins and live for righteousness; by his wounds you have been healed."

This verse directly references Isaiah 53:5, highlighting the substitutionary and atoning nature of Jesus' death.

Jesus' Burial and Resurrection

Matthew 27:57-60 (NIV): "As evening approached, there came a rich man from Arimathea, named Joseph, who had himself become a disciple of Jesus. Going to Pilate, he asked for Jesus' body, and Pilate ordered that it be given to him. Joseph took the body, wrapped it in a clean linen cloth, and placed it in his own new tomb that he had cut out of the rock. He rolled a big stone in front of the entrance to the tomb and went away."

Isaiah 53:9 is fulfilled in Jesus' burial in a rich man's tomb, despite His execution among criminals.

Comprehensive Commentary

Isaiah 53 is a remarkable prophecy that provides a detailed account of the Messiah's suffering, rejection, and ultimate purpose. The New Testament writers consistently reference this passage to affirm Jesus as the fulfillment of the

Suffering Servant. Through His life, death, and resurrection, Jesus embodied the sacrificial lamb who takes away the sin of the world.

Matthew Henry comments: "Isaiah 53 is the gospel in the Old Testament, revealing the heart of God's redemptive plan through the suffering and sacrifice of His Servant. Every detail of this prophecy points to Christ, the Lamb of God, who takes away the sin of the world."

John Calvin, in his Institutes of the Christian Religion, writes: "The prophecy of Isaiah 53 is a clear and incontrovertible testimony to the atoning work of Christ. It reveals the necessity and efficacy of His sacrifice, by which He bore the sins of many and secured the justification of all who believe in Him."

Theological Significance

1. Substitutionary Aton

ement: Isaiah 53 emphasizes the vicarious nature of the Servant's suffering, highlighting Jesus' role in bearing the punishment for humanity's sins.

2. Fulfillment of Prophecy: The detailed fulfillment of Isaiah's prophecy in the life of Jesus affirms the reliability and divine inspiration of Scripture.

3. Revelation of God's Love: The sacrificial death of Jesus reveals the depth of God's love for humanity, willing to endure immense suffering for the sake of our redemption.

4. Call to Faith and Repentance: The Suffering Servant's sacrifice calls believers to respond in faith, acknowledging their sins and accepting the forgiveness offered through Jesus Christ.

Conclusion

Isaiah 53 provides a profound and detailed prophecy about the suffering and sacrifice of the Messiah, fulfilled in the person and work of Jesus Christ. Through His rejection, suffering, and atoning death, Jesus embodied the role of the Suffering Servant, bearing the sins of many and securing salvation for all who believe.

As we reflect on this prophecy and its fulfillment, we are called to a deeper appreciation of Jesus' sacrificial love and the profound significance of His atoning work. This chapter has explored Isaiah's detailed prophecy and its fulfillment in Jesus, offering a comprehensive understanding of the theological implications and enduring relevance of the Suffering Servant.

The Sacrificial Lamb – The Crucifixion and Its Significance in Fulfilling Isaiah's Prophecy

Introduction

The crucifixion of Jesus Christ stands at the heart of Christian theology, marking the pivotal moment of redemption for humanity. This event is deeply rooted in Old Testament prophecies, particularly those found in Isaiah 53. In this chapter, we will explore the details of the crucifixion and its profound significance in fulfilling Isaiah's prophecy. Through an expository study and comprehensive commentary supported by Strong's Concordance, we will uncover the layers of meaning and divine purpose behind the crucifixion of Jesus.

Isaiah's Prophecy of the Suffering Servant

Isaiah 53 (NIV):

1. Who has believed our message and to whom has the arm of the Lord been revealed?

- The arm of the Lord signifies God's power and salvation. The disbelief of many in the Servant's mission underscores the unexpected nature of God's redemption plan (Strong's Concordance H2220, "זְרוֹעַ" - zĕrowaʿ, meaning arm or power).

2. He grew up before him like a tender shoot, and like a root out of dry ground. He had no beauty or majesty to attract us to him, nothing in his appearance that we should desire him.

- The humble and unassuming nature of the Servant reflects Jesus' earthly life, devoid of outward grandeur (Strong's Concordance H3126, "יוֹנֵק" - yonek, meaning a tender plant).

3. He was despised and rejected by mankind, a man of suffering, and familiar with pain. Like one from whom people hide their faces he was despised, and we held him in low esteem.

- Jesus' rejection and suffering are vividly portrayed here, emphasizing His identification with human pain and sorrow (Strong's Concordance H2534, "חֵמָה" - chemah, meaning wrath or indignation).

4. Surely he took up our pain and bore our suffering, yet we considered him punished by God, stricken by him, and afflicted.

- The substitutionary nature of Jesus' suffering is highlighted, as He bears the pain and punishment meant for others (Strong's Concordance H6031, "עָנָה" - anah, meaning to afflict or humble).

5. But he was pierced for our transgressions, he was crushed for our iniquities; the punishment that brought us peace was on him, and by his wounds we are healed.

- The crucifixion directly fulfills this verse, with Jesus being physically pierced and bearing the punishment for humanity's sins (Strong's Concordance H2490, "חָלַל" - chalal, meaning to pierce or wound).

6. We all, like sheep, have gone astray, each of us has turned to our own way; and the Lord has laid on him the iniquity of us all.

- Humanity's collective waywardness is contrasted with the Servant's role in bearing these iniquities (Strong's Concordance H5771, "עָוֹן" - avon, meaning iniquity or guilt).

7. He was oppressed and afflicted, yet he did not open his mouth; he was led like a lamb to the slaughter, and as a sheep before its shearers is silent, so he did not open his mouth.

- Jesus' silent submission during His trial and crucifixion fulfills this prophetic imagery (Strong's Concordance H3533, "כָּבַשׁ" - kabash, meaning to subdue or silence).

8. By oppression and judgment he was taken away. Yet who of his generation protested? For he was cut off from the land of the living; for the transgression of my people he was punished.

- The unjust treatment and death of Jesus are depicted, showing His suffering as a result of bearing the sins of others (Strong's Concordance H1504, "גָּזַר" - gazar, meaning to cut off or divide).

9. He was assigned a grave with the wicked, and with the rich in his death, though he had done no violence, nor was any deceit in his mouth.

- Despite His innocence, Jesus' death and burial align with this prophecy (Strong's Concordance H7563, "רָשָׁע" - rasha`, meaning wicked or guilty).

10. Yet it was the Lord's will to crush him and cause him to suffer, and though the Lord makes his life an offering for sin, he will see his offspring and prolong his days, and the will of the Lord will prosper in his hand.

- Jesus' suffering is part of God's redemptive plan, with the promise of future vindication and prosperity (Strong's Concordance H6213, "עָשָׂה" - asah, meaning to do or make).

11. After he has suffered, he will see the light of life and be satisfied; by his knowledge my righteous servant will justify many, and he will bear their iniquities.

- The resurrection and justification of many through Jesus' sacrifice are foretold here (Strong's Concordance H6663, "צָדַק" - tsadaq, meaning to be righteous or just).

12. Therefore I will give him a portion among the great, and he will divide the spoils with the strong, because he poured out his life unto death, and was numbered with the

transgressors. For he bore the sin of many, and made intercession for the transgressors.

- Jesus' exaltation and reward for His sacrificial death and intercession are prophesied (Strong's Concordance H7725, "שׁוּב" - shuwb, meaning to return or restore).

The Crucifixion of Jesus

The crucifixion is the culmination of Jesus' earthly ministry, fulfilling Isaiah's prophecy in profound and precise detail. The New Testament provides a comprehensive account of this event, highlighting its theological significance and its role in God's redemptive plan.

The Trial and Condemnation

Matthew 27:11-26 (NIV):

"Meanwhile Jesus stood before the governor, and the governor asked him, 'Are you the king of the Jews?' 'You have said so,' Jesus replied. When he was accused by the chief priests and the elders, he gave no answer. Then Pilate asked him, 'Don't you hear the testimony they are bringing against you?' But Jesus made no reply, not even to a single charge—to the great amazement of the governor."

Analysis

1. Silent Before Accusers: Jesus' silence during His trial fulfills Isaiah 53:7, emphasizing His meekness and

submission (Strong's Concordance G4623, "σιγάω" - sigaō, meaning to be silent).

2. Unjust Judgment: The unjust condemnation of Jesus aligns with Isaiah 53:8, where the Servant is oppressed and judged unfairly (Strong's Concordance G2919, "κρίνω" - krinō, meaning to judge).

The Crucifixion

Matthew 27:32-50 (NIV):

"As they were going out, they met a man from Cyrene, named Simon, and they forced him to carry the cross. They came to a place called Golgotha (which means 'the place of the skull'). There they offered Jesus wine to drink, mixed with gall; but after tasting it, he refused to drink it. When they had crucified him, they divided up his clothes by casting lots. And sitting down, they kept watch over him there. Above his head they placed the written charge against him: this is jesus, the king of the jews. Two rebels were crucified with him, one on his right and one on his left. Those who passed by hurled insults at him, shaking their heads and saying, 'You who are going to destroy the temple and build it in three days, save yourself! Come down from the cross, if you are the Son of God!' In the same way the chief priests, the teachers of the law and the elders mocked him. 'He saved others,' they said, 'but he can't save himself! He's the king of Israel! Let him come down now from the cross, and we will believe in him. He trusts in God. Let God rescue him now if he wants him, for he said, "I am the Son of God."' In the same way the rebels who were crucified with him also heaped insults on him. From noon until three in the afternoon darkness came over all the land. About three in the afternoon Jesus cried out in a loud voice, 'Eli, Eli, lema sabachthani?' (which means 'My God, my God, why have you forsaken me?'). When some of those standing there heard this, they said, 'He's calling Elijah.' Immediately one of them ran and got a sponge. He filled it with wine vinegar, put it on a staff, and offered it to Jesus to drink. The rest said, 'Now leave him alone. Let's see if Elijah comes to save him.' And when Jesus had cried out again in a loud voice, he gave up his spirit."

Analysis

1. Crucifixion: The act of crucifixion fulfills the piercing and crushing described in Isaiah 53:5 (Strong's Concordance G4717, "σταυρόω" - stauroō, meaning to crucify).

2. Division of Garments: The soldiers casting lots for Jesus' clothes fulfills Psalm 22:18 and aligns with the imagery of the Servant being deprived (Strong's Concordance G2819, "κλῆρος" - klēros, meaning lot).

3. Mockery and Insults: The mocking of Jesus by onlookers fulfills the prophecy of the Servant being despised and rejected (Strong's Concordance G987, "βλασφημέω" - blasphēmeō, meaning to blaspheme or insult).

4. Darkness: The darkness over the land signifies the profound significance of this moment, aligning with the cosmic implications of the Servant's suffering (Strong's Concordance G4655, "σκότος" - skotos, meaning darkness).

5. Jesus' Cry of Forsakenness: Jesus' cry, "My God, my God, why have you forsaken me?" quotes Psalm 22:1 and underscores the depth of His suffering and identification with human anguish (Strong's Concordance G1459, "ἐγκαταλείπω" - egkataleipō, meaning to forsake or abandon).

Theological Significance

1. Substitutionary Atonement: Jesus' crucifixion fulfills Isaiah's prophecy of the Servant bearing the sins of many. His death serves as a substitute for humanity, taking the punishment that we deserve (1 Peter 2:24).

2. Fulfillment of Prophecy: The detailed fulfillment of Isaiah's prophecy in the crucifixion of Jesus affirms the reliability and divine inspiration of Scripture. Every aspect of Jesus' suffering and death was foretold, highlighting God's sovereign plan (Luke 24:25-27).

3. Revelation of God's Love: The crucifixion reveals the depth of God's love for humanity, as He willingly endures immense suffering to redeem us. This act of sacrificial love calls us to respond in faith and gratitude (John 3:16).

4. Victory Over Sin and Death: Jesus' death and subsequent resurrection signify His victory over sin and death, providing a basis for our hope and salvation. The Servant's suffering leads to ultimate triumph and restoration (Romans 6:9-10).

5. Call to Discipleship: The crucifixion also calls believers to take up their own crosses, following Jesus' example of self-sacrifice and obedience to God (Matthew 16:24).

Comprehensive Commentary

Matthew Henry comments: "The crucifixion of Christ is the fulfillment of Isaiah's prophecy in the most literal and profound sense. It shows us the suffering Servant who bears our sins, the Lamb of God who takes away the sin of the world. Every detail of His passion was foretold, and every suffering He endured was for our redemption."

John Calvin, in his Institutes of the Christian Religion, writes: "The prophecy of Isaiah 53 finds its full realization in the crucifixion of Christ. Here we see the depths of God's mercy and justice, the confluence of His love and righteousness. The Servant's suffering was necessary to secure our salvation, to satisfy divine justice, and to reconcile us to God."

Conclusion

The crucifixion of Jesus Christ is the pivotal event that fulfills Isaiah's detailed prophecy of the Suffering Servant. Through His suffering, rejection, and death, Jesus bore the sins of humanity, providing the means for our redemption and reconciliation with God. This chapter has explored the crucifixion in the light of Isaiah 53, highlighting the profound theological significance and the fulfillment of God's redemptive plan.

As we reflect on the crucifixion, we are called to a deeper appreciation of Jesus' sacrificial love and the immense cost of our salvation. The fulfillment of Isaiah's prophecy in the crucifixion of Jesus affirms the reliability of Scripture and the sovereignty of God's plan, inviting us to respond in faith, gratitude, and commitment to follow Him.

The Atonement – Theological Implications of Jesus' Sacrifice for Sin

The atonement of Jesus Christ is central to Christian theology, encompassing the reconciliation between God and humanity through Jesus' sacrificial death. This chapter will explore the theological implications of Jesus' sacrifice for sin, using Bible verses and expository study supported by Strong's Concordance and comprehensive commentary. We will examine how Jesus' atonement fulfills Old Testament prophecies, addresses the problem of sin, and establishes the foundation for salvation and eternal life.

The Necessity of Atonement

Romans 3:23-25 (NIV): "For all have sinned and fall short of the glory of God, and all are justified freely by his grace through the redemption that came by Christ Jesus. God presented Christ as a sacrifice of atonement, through the shedding of his blood—to be received by faith. He did this to demonstrate his righteousness, because in his forbearance he had left the sins committed beforehand unpunished."

Analysis

1. Universality of Sin: All humanity has sinned and fallen short of God's glory, necessitating atonement (Strong's Concordance G264, "ἁμαρτία" - hamartia, meaning sin).

2. Justification by Grace: Justification is a free gift of God's grace, accomplished through Jesus' redemptive work (Strong's Concordance G1343, "δικαιοσύνη" - dikaiosynē, meaning righteousness).

3. Sacrifice of Atonement: Jesus is presented as the sacrifice of atonement, emphasizing His role in reconciling humanity to God through His blood (Strong's Concordance

G2435, "ἱλαστήριον" - hilastērion, meaning propitiation or atoning sacrifice).

4. Demonstration of Righteousness: God's righteousness is demonstrated through the atonement, showing His justice in dealing with sin (Strong's Concordance G1343, "δικαιοσύνη" - dikaiosynē, meaning righteousness).

Fulfillment of Old Testament Prophecies

Isaiah 53:5-6 (NIV): "But he was pierced for our transgressions, he was crushed for our iniquities; the punishment that brought us peace was on him, and by his wounds we are healed. We all, like sheep, have gone astray, each of us has turned to our own way; and the Lord has laid on him the iniquity of us all."

Analysis

1. Pierced for Transgressions: Jesus' crucifixion fulfills the prophecy of being pierced for our sins (Strong's Concordance H2490, "חָלַל" - chalal, meaning to pierce or wound).

2. Crushed for Iniquities: The severity of Jesus' suffering is emphasized, reflecting the weight of humanity's sins (Strong's Concordance H1792, "דָּכָא" - daka', meaning to crush or oppress).

3. Punishment for Peace: Jesus' punishment brings us peace with God, highlighting the substitutionary nature of His

atonement (Strong's Concordance H4148, "מוּסָר" - musar, meaning discipline or chastisement).

4. Healing by His Wounds: The healing brought by Jesus' wounds signifies both physical and spiritual restoration (Strong's Concordance H2250, "חַבּוּרָה" - chabburah, meaning stripe or wound).

Addressing the Problem of Sin

Romans 6:23 (NIV): "For the wages of sin is death, but the gift of God is eternal life in Christ Jesus our Lord."

Analysis

1. Wages of Sin: Sin results in death, indicating the serious consequences of disobedience to God (Strong's Concordance G3800, "ὀψώνιον" - opsōnion, meaning wages or reward).

2. Gift of God: Eternal life is presented as a gift from God, contrasting the deserved wages of sin (Strong's Concordance G5486, "χάρισμα" - charisma, meaning gift of grace).

3. Eternal Life in Christ: This gift is realized through Jesus Christ, emphasizing His role as the source of salvation (Strong's Concordance G166, "αἰώνιος" - aiōnios, meaning eternal).

The Nature of Atonement

1 John 2:2 (NIV): "He is the atoning sacrifice for our sins, and not only for ours but also for the sins of the whole world."

Analysis

1. Atoning Sacrifice: Jesus is the propitiation for our sins, satisfying the wrath of God and reconciling us to Him (Strong's Concordance G2434, "ἱλασμός" - hilasmos, meaning propitiation).

2. For the Whole World: The universal scope of Jesus' atonement is emphasized, extending beyond individual sins to encompass the entire world (Strong's Concordance G2889, "κόσμος" - kosmos, meaning world or universe).

Theological Implications

1. Substitutionary Atonement: Jesus' death was a substitutionary sacrifice, taking the place of sinners and bearing the punishment that we deserved. This is central to the Christian understanding of atonement (Isaiah 53:5; 1 Peter 3:18).

2. Reconciliation with God: The atonement restores the broken relationship between God and humanity, allowing us to be reconciled to God through Jesus Christ (2 Corinthians 5:18-19).

3. Justification by Faith: Through Jesus' atonement, believers are justified by faith, declared righteous before God

not because of their own merits but because of Jesus' sacrifice (Romans 3:24-26).

4. Redemption and Forgiveness: The atonement secures redemption and forgiveness of sins, freeing believers from the bondage of sin and granting them a new life in Christ (Ephesians 1:7).

5. Propitiation and Expiation: Jesus' sacrifice serves as propitiation (satisfying God's wrath) and expiation (removing our sins), fully addressing the problem of sin and its consequences (1 John 2:2; Romans 3:25).

6. New Covenant: The atonement establishes the new covenant, in which God's law is written on our hearts and we receive the indwelling of the Holy Spirit (Hebrews 9:15; Jeremiah 31:31-34).

7. Victory Over Sin and Death: Jesus' atonement not only deals with the guilt of sin but also breaks its power, enabling believers to live in victory over sin and death (Romans 6:10-11).

Comprehensive Commentary

Matthew Henry comments: "The atonement of Christ is the central theme of the gospel, providing the foundation for our salvation. Through His sacrificial death, Jesus bore the punishment for our sins, satisfied the demands of divine justice, and opened the way for our reconciliation with God."

John Calvin, in his Institutes of the Christian Religion, writes: "The atonement of Christ is the apex of God's redemptive plan, demonstrating His justice and mercy. By taking our place and bearing our sins, Christ secured our justification and reconciliation, ensuring that all who believe in Him are accepted and forgiven."

Conclusion

The atonement of Jesus Christ is the cornerstone of Christian faith, addressing the problem of sin and providing the means for reconciliation with God. Through His sacrificial death, Jesus fulfilled the Old Testament prophecies, bore the punishment for our sins, and secured our salvation. The theological implications of the atonement are profound, encompassing substitutionary atonement, justification by faith, redemption, and the establishment of the new covenant.

As we reflect on the atonement, we are called to respond in faith, gratitude, and obedience, recognizing the immense cost of our salvation and the depth of God's love for us. This chapter has explored the theological significance of Jesus' sacrifice for sin, offering a comprehensive understanding of its implications for our lives and our relationship with God.

The Correlation Between Isaiah's Prophecy and New Testament Teachings on Atonement

The prophetic vision of the Suffering Servant in Isaiah 53 is one of the most significant passages in the Old Testament, foreshadowing the atoning work of Jesus Christ. The New Testament writings frequently reference Isaiah's prophecy to explain and affirm the atonement accomplished through Jesus' life, death, and resurrection. This chapter will explore the correlation between Isaiah's prophecy and New Testament teachings on atonement, examining key texts and their theological implications. Through an expository study supported by Strong's Concordance and comprehensive commentary, we will uncover the deep connections between these two parts of Scripture.

Isaiah's Prophecy of the Suffering Servant

Isaiah 53:3-6 (NIV):

"He was despised and rejected by mankind, a man of suffering, and familiar with pain. Like one from whom people hide their faces he was despised, and we held him in low esteem. Surely he took up our pain and bore our suffering, yet we considered him punished by God, stricken by him, and afflicted. But he was pierced for our transgressions, he was crushed for our iniquities; the punishment that brought us peace was on him, and by his wounds we are healed. We all, like sheep, have gone astray, each of us has turned to our own way; and the Lord has laid on him the iniquity of us all."

Analysis

1. Despised and Rejected: The Servant's rejection by humanity highlights His identification with human suffering and alienation (Strong's Concordance H959, "בָּזָה" - bazah, meaning to despise or disdain).

2. Bearing Our Pain and Suffering: The Servant's vicarious suffering is emphasized, showing His role in taking on humanity's pain and suffering (Strong's Concordance H5445, "סָבַל" - sabal, meaning to bear or carry).

3. Pierced for Our Transgressions: The prophecy clearly indicates that the Servant will be physically pierced and crushed as a substitute for human sin (Strong's Concordance H2490, "חָלַל" - chalal, meaning to pierce or wound).

4. Punishment for Peace: The Servant's suffering brings peace and healing, highlighting the redemptive purpose of His sacrifice (Strong's Concordance H4148, "מוּסָר" - musar, meaning discipline or chastisement).

5. Iniquity Laid on Him: The totality of human sin is placed upon the Servant, underscoring the comprehensive nature of His atonement (Strong's Concordance H5771, "עָוֹן" - avon, meaning iniquity or guilt).

Fulfillment in the New Testament

The New Testament writers explicitly connect the life and work of Jesus with Isaiah's prophecy, affirming that Jesus is the fulfillment of the Suffering Servant and the agent of atonement.

Jesus as the Suffering Servant

Matthew 8:16-17 (NIV):

"When evening came, many who were demon-possessed were brought to him, and he drove out the spirits with a word and healed all the sick. This was to fulfill what was spoken through the prophet Isaiah: 'He took up our infirmities and bore our diseases.'"

Analysis

1. Healing and Deliverance: Jesus' healing ministry is seen as a fulfillment of Isaiah's prophecy, highlighting His role in bearing physical and spiritual burdens (Strong's Concordance G941, "βαστάζω" - bastazō, meaning to bear or carry).

2. Fulfillment of Prophecy: The quotation from Isaiah 53:4 demonstrates the New Testament writers' understanding of Jesus as the Suffering Servant (Strong's Concordance G4137, "πληρόω" - plēroō, meaning to fulfill).

Atonement through Jesus' Sacrifice

1 Peter 2:24 (NIV):

"He himself bore our sins in his body on the cross, so that we might die to sins and live for righteousness; by his wounds you have been healed."

Analysis

1. Bearing Our Sins: Jesus' act of bearing sins on the cross directly correlates with Isaiah 53:4-5, emphasizing the substitutionary nature of His atonement (Strong's Concordance G3991, "προσήλυτος" - prosēlytos, meaning convert or proselyte).

2. Healing through Wounds: The healing brought by Jesus' wounds is a fulfillment of Isaiah's prophecy, showing the redemptive power of His suffering (Strong's Concordance G2390, "ἰάομαι" - iaomai, meaning to heal).

The Purpose of Jesus' Suffering

Romans 4:25 (NIV):

"He was delivered over to death for our sins and was raised to life for our justification."

Analysis

1. Delivered for Our Sins: Jesus' death is explicitly linked to the purpose of bearing human sin, fulfilling Isaiah's description of the Servant (Strong's Concordance G3860, "παραδίδωμι" - paradidōmi, meaning to deliver or hand over).

2. Raised for Our Justification: Jesus' resurrection is tied to our justification, affirming the complete work of atonement (Strong's Concordance G1344, "δικαιόω" - dikaioō, meaning to justify).

The Scope of Jesus' Atonement

1 John 2:2 (NIV):

"He is the atoning sacrifice for our sins, and not only for ours but also for the sins of the whole world."

Analysis

1. Atoning Sacrifice: Jesus is described as the propitiation for sins, aligning with Isaiah's portrayal of the Servant's sacrificial role (Strong's Concordance G2434, "ἱλασμός" - hilasmos, meaning propitiation).

2. Universal Scope: The atonement extends beyond individual sins to encompass the entire world, reflecting the comprehensive nature of the Servant's sacrifice (Strong's Concordance G2889, "κόσμος" - kosmos, meaning world or universe).

Theological Implications

1. Substitutionary Atonement: Both Isaiah and the New Testament emphasize the substitutionary nature of Jesus' atonement. He took the punishment meant for us, bearing our sins and iniquities (Isaiah 53:5; 1 Peter 2:24).

2. Reconciliation with God: The atonement restores the broken relationship between God and humanity, allowing us to be reconciled to God through Jesus Christ (2 Corinthians 5:18-19).

3. Justification by Faith: Through Jesus' atonement, believers are justified by faith, declared righteous before God not because of their own merits but because of Jesus' sacrifice (Romans 3:24-26).

4. Redemption and Forgiveness: The atonement secures redemption and forgiveness of sins, freeing believers from the bondage of sin and granting them a new life in Christ (Ephesians 1:7).

5. Propitiation and Expiation: Jesus' sacrifice serves as propitiation (satisfying God's wrath) and expiation (removing our sins), fully addressing the problem of sin and its consequences (1 John 2:2; Romans 3:25).

6. New Covenant: The atonement establishes the new covenant, in which God's law is written on our hearts and we receive the indwelling of the Holy Spirit (Hebrews 9:15; Jeremiah 31:31-34).

7. Victory Over Sin and Death: Jesus' atonement not only deals with the guilt of sin but also breaks its power, enabling believers to live in victory over sin and death (Romans 6:10-11).

Comprehensive Commentary

Matthew Henry comments: "The atonement of Christ is the central theme of the gospel, providing the foundation for our salvation. Through His sacrificial death, Jesus bore the punishment for our sins, satisfied the demands of divine justice, and opened the way for our reconciliation with God."

John Calvin, in his Institutes of the Christian Religion, writes: "The atonement of Christ is the apex of God's redemptive plan, demonstrating His justice and mercy. By taking our place and bearing our sins, Christ secured our justification and reconciliation, ensuring that all who believe in Him are accepted and forgiven."

Conclusion

The correlation between Isaiah's prophecy and New Testament teachings on atonement is profound and deeply interconnected. Isaiah 53 provides a detailed and vivid prophecy of the Suffering Servant, fulfilled in the life, death, and resurrection of Jesus Christ. The New Testament writers explicitly connect Jesus' atoning work with Isaiah's prophecy, affirming that Jesus is the fulfillment of the Suffering Servant and the agent of atonement.

As we reflect on the atonement, we are called to a deeper appreciation of Jesus' sacrificial love and the immense cost of our salvation. The fulfillment of Isaiah's prophecy in the atonement of Jesus affirms the reliability of Scripture and the sovereignty of God's plan, inviting us to respond in faith, gratitude, and commitment to follow Him. This chapter has explored the theological significance of Jesus' sacrifice for sin, offering a comprehensive understanding of its implications for our lives and our relationship with God.

THE RESURRECTION AND ETERNITY KINGSHIP – THE EMPTY TOMB

The resurrection of Jesus Christ is the cornerstone of Christian faith, marking His victory over sin and death and affirming His identity as the Son of God. The accounts of the empty tomb in the Gospels provide compelling evidence for the resurrection and offer profound theological insights. This chapter will examine the accounts of Jesus' resurrection in Matthew 28, Mark 16, Luke 24, and John 20. Through an expository study supported by Strong's Concordance and comprehensive commentary, we will explore the details and significance of the resurrection.

The Resurrection Account in Matthew

Matthew 28:1-10 (NIV):

"After the Sabbath, at dawn on the first day of the week, Mary Magdalene and the other Mary went to look at the tomb. There was a violent earthquake, for an angel of the Lord came down from heaven and, going to the tomb, rolled back the stone and sat on it. His appearance was like lightning, and his clothes were white as snow. The guards were so afraid of him that they shook and became like dead men. The angel said to the women, 'Do not be afraid, for I know that you are looking for Jesus, who was crucified. He is not here; he has risen, just as he said. Come and see the place where he lay. Then go quickly and tell his disciples: "He has risen from the dead and is going ahead of you into Galilee. There you will see him." Now I have told you.' So the women hurried away from the tomb, afraid yet filled with joy, and ran to tell his disciples. Suddenly Jesus met them. 'Greetings,' he said. They came to him, clasped his feet and worshiped him. Then Jesus said to them, 'Do not be afraid. Go and tell my brothers to go to Galilee; there they will see me.'"

Analysis

1. The Visit of the Women: Mary Magdalene and the other Mary are the first to visit the tomb, highlighting the role of women in the resurrection narrative (Strong's Concordance G3137, "Μαρία" - Maria, meaning Mary).

2. The Earthquake and Angel: The violent earthquake and the angel's appearance signify divine intervention and the power of God (Strong's Concordance G4578, "σεισμός" - seismos, meaning earthquake).

3. The Empty Tomb: The angel's declaration, "He is not here; he has risen," confirms the resurrection, fulfilling Jesus' own predictions (Strong's Concordance G1453, "ἐγείρω" - egeirō, meaning to raise up).

4. The Women's Response: The women's mixture of fear and joy reflects the awe-inspiring nature of the resurrection (Strong's Concordance G5401, "φόβος" - phobos, meaning fear; G5479, "χαρά" - chara, meaning joy).

5. Jesus' Appearance: Jesus' greeting and the women's worship emphasize His bodily resurrection and divine authority (Strong's Concordance G4352, "προσκυνέω" - proskyneō, meaning to worship).

The Resurrection Account in Mark

Mark 16:1-8 (NIV):

"When the Sabbath was over, Mary Magdalene, Mary the mother of James, and Salome bought spices so that they might go to anoint Jesus' body. Very early on the first day of the week, just after sunrise, they were on their way to the tomb and they asked each other, 'Who will roll the stone away from the entrance of the tomb?' But when they looked up, they saw that the stone, which was very large, had been rolled away. As they entered the tomb, they saw a young man dressed in a white robe sitting on the right side, and they were alarmed. 'Don't be alarmed,' he said. 'You are looking for Jesus the Nazarene, who was crucified. He has risen! He is not here. See the place where they laid him. But go, tell his disciples and Peter, "He is going ahead of you into Galilee. There you will see him, just as he told you."' Trembling and bewildered, the women went out and fled from the tomb. They said nothing to anyone, because they were afraid."

Analysis

1. The Visit of the Women: The inclusion of Salome adds another witness to the resurrection account (Strong's Concordance G4539, "Σαλώμη" - Salōmē, meaning Salome).

2. The Rolled-Away Stone: The large stone rolled away signifies divine intervention, as it was too large for the women to move themselves (Strong's Concordance G3037, "λίθος" - lithos, meaning stone).

3. The Angelic Message: The young man in a white robe, identified as an angel, delivers the message of Jesus' resurrection (Strong's Concordance G32, "ἄγγελος" - angelos, meaning angel).

4. Trembling and Bewilderment: The women's reaction of trembling and bewilderment underscores the

extraordinary nature of the resurrection event (Strong's Concordance G5156, "τρομος" - tromos, meaning trembling).

The Resurrection Account in Luke

Luke 24:1-12 (NIV):

"On the first day of the week, very early in the morning, the women took the spices they had prepared and went to the tomb. They found the stone rolled away from the tomb, but when they entered, they did not find the body of the Lord Jesus. While they were wondering about this, suddenly two men in clothes that gleamed like lightning stood beside them. In their fright the women bowed down with their faces to the ground, but the men said to them, 'Why do you look for the living among the dead? He is not here; he has risen! Remember how he told you, while he was still with you in Galilee: "The Son of Man must be delivered over to the hands of sinners, be crucified and on the third day be raised again."' Then they remembered his words. When they came back from the tomb, they told all these things to the Eleven and to all the others. It was Mary Magdalene, Joanna, Mary the mother of James, and the others with them who told this to the apostles. But they did not believe the women, because their words seemed to them like nonsense. Peter, however, got up and ran to the tomb. Bending over, he saw the strips of linen lying by themselves, and he went away, wondering to himself what had happened."

Analysis

1. Multiple Witnesses: The presence of multiple women, including Joanna, adds credibility to the resurrection account (Strong's Concordance G2489, "Ἰωάννα" - Iōanna, meaning Joanna).

2. Two Angels: The appearance of two angels, whose clothes gleamed like lightning, emphasizes the divine confirmation of the resurrection (Strong's Concordance G32, "ἄγγελος" - angelos, meaning angel).

3. The Reminder of Jesus' Words: The angels remind the women of Jesus' prophecy about His death and resurrection, highlighting the fulfillment of His words (Strong's Concordance G3415, "μιμνήσκομαι" - mimnēskomai, meaning to remember).

4. Peter's Investigation: Peter's visit to the tomb and his amazement underline the initial disbelief and subsequent realization of the resurrection (Strong's Concordance G2296, "θαυμάζω" - thaumazō, meaning to wonder or be amazed).

The Resurrection Account in John

John 20:1-18 (NIV):

"Early on the first day of the week, while it was still dark, Mary Magdalene went to the tomb and saw that the stone had been removed from the entrance. So she came running to Simon Peter and the other disciple, the one Jesus loved, and said, 'They have taken the Lord out of the tomb, and we don't know where they have put him!' So Peter and the other disciple started for the tomb. Both were running, but the other disciple outran Peter and reached the tomb first. He bent over and looked in at the strips of linen lying there but did not go in. Then Simon Peter came along behind him and went straight into the tomb. He saw the strips of linen lying there, as well as the cloth that had been wrapped around Jesus' head. The cloth was still lying in its place, separate from the linen. Finally the other disciple, who had reached the tomb first, also went inside. He saw and believed. (They still did not understand from Scripture that Jesus had to rise from the dead.) Then the disciples went back to where they were staying. Now Mary stood outside the tomb crying. As she wept, she bent over to look into the tomb and saw two angels in white, seated where Jesus' body had been, one at the head and the other at the foot. They asked her, 'Woman, why are you crying?' 'They have taken my Lord away,' she said, 'and I don't know where they have put him.' At this, she turned around and saw Jesus standing there, but she did not realize that it was Jesus. He asked her, 'Woman, why are you crying? Who is it you are looking for?' Thinking he was the gardener, she said, 'Sir, if you have carried him away, tell me where you have put him, and I will get him.' Jesus said to her, 'Mary.' She turned toward him and cried out in Aramaic, 'Rabboni!' (which means

'Teacher'). Jesus said, 'Do not hold on to me, for I have not yet ascended to the Father. Go instead to my brothers and tell them, "I am ascending to my Father and your Father, to my God and your God."' Mary Magdalene went to the disciples with the news: 'I have seen the Lord!' And she told them that he had said these things to her."

Analysis

1. Mary Magdalene's Visit: Mary Magdalene's early visit to the tomb highlights her devotion and the significance of her witness (Strong's Concordance G3137, "Μαρία" - Maria, meaning Mary).

2. The Strips of Linen: The presence of the linen strips and the separate cloth around Jesus' head suggest a resurrection rather than a body theft (Strong's Concordance G3608, "ὀθόνιον" - othonion, meaning linen cloth).

3. Belief and Misunderstanding: The disciples' initial belief in the resurrection, despite their lack of understanding from Scripture, underscores the transformative impact of the empty tomb (Strong's Concordance G4100, "πιστεύω" - pisteuō, meaning to believe)

4. Jesus' Appearance to Mary: Jesus' personal appearance to Mary and His commissioning her to tell the disciples highlight the importance of her testimony (Strong's Concordance G3700, "ὀπτάνομαι" - optanomai, meaning to appear).

Theological Significance of the Resurrection

1. Victory Over Death: The resurrection signifies Jesus' victory over death, providing the foundation for Christian hope in eternal life (1 Corinthians 15:54-57).

2. Confirmation of Jesus' Divinity: The resurrection affirms Jesus' identity as the Son of God, validating His teachings and claims (Romans 1:4).

3. Firstfruits of the Resurrection: Jesus is the "firstfruits" of those who have fallen asleep, guaranteeing the future resurrection of believers (1 Corinthians 15:20).

4. Foundation for Justification: The resurrection is essential for our justification, demonstrating that God accepted Jesus' sacrifice on our behalf (Romans 4:25).

5. Empowerment for Mission: The risen Jesus commissions His disciples to spread the gospel, emphasizing the global mission of the church (Matthew 28:18-20).

Comprehensive Commentary

Matthew Henry comments: "The resurrection of Christ is the cornerstone of our faith. It provides the firm foundation upon which our hope of eternal life is built. The empty tomb is a powerful testament to the victory of Christ over sin and death, and the assurance of our own resurrection."

John Calvin, in his Institutes of the Christian Religion, writes: "The resurrection of Christ is the primary article of our faith. It is the culmination of the gospel, ensuring that our justification is complete and our salvation secure. Through the resurrection, we see the power of God manifested and the promise of eternal life assured."

Conclusion

The accounts of Jesus' resurrection in Matthew, Mark, Luke, and John provide a comprehensive and harmonious testimony to the central event of the Christian faith. Each Gospel emphasizes different aspects of the resurrection, but all converge on the fundamental truth that Jesus has risen from the dead, confirming His identity as the Son of God and securing the hope of eternal life for all who believe.

The theological significance of the resurrection is profound, encompassing victory over death, confirmation of Jesus' divinity, assurance of future resurrection, foundation for justification, and empowerment for mission. As we reflect on the resurrection, we are called to live in the light of this transformative event, proclaiming the risen Christ and embracing the hope and power that His resurrection brings.

This chapter has explored the resurrection accounts in the Gospels, offering an expository study and comprehensive commentary on the empty tomb and its significance. The resurrection is not only a historical event but also the foundation of our faith and the guarantee of our future hope.

Isaiah's Hints at the Resurrection and Eternal Life

The concept of resurrection and eternal life is a cornerstone of Christian eschatology. While the New Testament provides explicit teachings on these themes, the Old Testament also contains hints and anticipations of the resurrection. Isaiah 26:19 is a pivotal verse in this regard, offering a prophetic glimpse into the hope of resurrection and eternal life. This chapter will explore Isaiah's hints at the resurrection and eternal life, focusing on Isaiah 26:19, and how this prophecy correlates with New Testament teachings. Through an expository study supported by Strong's Concordance and comprehensive commentary, we will uncover the profound significance of this verse.

Isaiah 26:19 – A Prophetic Hint of Resurrection

Isaiah 26:19 (NIV):

"But your dead will live, Lord; their bodies will rise— let those who dwell in the dust wake up and shout for joy— your dew is like the dew of the morning; the earth will give birth to her dead."

Analysis

1. "Your dead will live": This statement proclaims the resurrection of the dead, affirming that those who have died will be brought back to life (Strong's Concordance H2421, "חָיָה" - chayah, meaning to live or revive).

2. "Their bodies will rise": The physical resurrection is emphasized, indicating that it is not merely a spiritual continuation but a bodily resurrection (Strong's Concordance H6965, "קוּם" - qum, meaning to rise or stand up).

3. "Let those who dwell in the dust wake up and shout for joy": The imagery of awakening from the dust suggests the resurrection from the grave, accompanied by joy and celebration (Strong's Concordance H5782, "עוּר" - ur, meaning to wake up or rouse).

4. "Your dew is like the dew of the morning": Dew symbolizes renewal and life, suggesting that God's power to resurrect is as natural and life-giving as the morning dew (Strong's Concordance H2919, "טַל" - tal, meaning dew).

5. "The earth will give birth to her dead": This metaphor of the earth giving birth emphasizes the certainty

and naturalness of the resurrection, as a mother giving birth to a child (Strong's Concordance H5307, "נָפַל" - naphal, meaning to fall or bring forth).

Correlation with New Testament Teachings

The New Testament writers expand on the themes of resurrection and eternal life, often drawing from the Old Testament to illustrate the fulfillment of these prophecies in Jesus Christ.

The Resurrection of Jesus

1 Corinthians 15:20-22 (NIV):

"But Christ has indeed been raised from the dead, the firstfruits of those who have fallen asleep. For since death came through a man, the resurrection of the dead comes also through a man. For as in Adam all die, so in Christ all will be made alive."

Analysis

1. Firstfruits of Those Who Have Fallen Asleep: Jesus' resurrection is described as the "firstfruits," indicating the first of many to follow, fulfilling the hope expressed in Isaiah 26:19 (Strong's Concordance G536, "ἀπαρχή" - aparchē, meaning firstfruits).

2. Resurrection Through a Man: Just as death entered the world through Adam, resurrection comes through Jesus, affirming the universal hope of resurrection (Strong's

Concordance G386, "ἀνάστασις" - anastasis, meaning resurrection).

3. In Christ All Will Be Made Alive: This universal promise echoes Isaiah's prophecy that the dead will live, emphasizing the comprehensive nature of resurrection in Christ (Strong's Concordance G2227, "ζωοποιέω" - zōopoieō, meaning to make alive).

The Promise of Eternal Life

John 11:25-26 (NIV):

"Jesus said to her, 'I am the resurrection and the life. The one who believes in me will live, even though they die; and whoever lives by believing in me will never die. Do you believe this?'"

Analysis

1. I Am the Resurrection and the Life: Jesus' declaration identifies Him as the source of both resurrection and eternal life, fulfilling the prophetic hope in Isaiah (Strong's Concordance G386, "ἀνάστασις" - anastasis, meaning resurrection).

2. The One Who Believes in Me Will Live: Belief in Jesus is the key to experiencing the resurrection and eternal life, connecting the faith of believers with the prophetic promises (Strong's Concordance G4100, "πιστεύω" - pisteuō, meaning to believe).

3. Will Never Die: The promise of eternal life means that physical death is not the end, but a transition to everlasting life, resonating with Isaiah's vision of life beyond death (Strong's Concordance G599, "ἀποθνῄσκω" - apothnēskō, meaning to die).

The Resurrection Body

Philippians 3:20-21 (NIV):

"But our citizenship is in heaven. And we eagerly await a Savior from there, the Lord Jesus Christ, who, by the power that enables him to bring everything under his control, will transform our lowly bodies so that they will be like his glorious body."

Analysis

1. Citizenship in Heaven: Believers' ultimate home is in heaven, where they await the return of Christ and the fulfillment of resurrection promises (Strong's Concordance G4175, "πολίτευμα" - politeuma, meaning citizenship).

2. Transformation of Lowly Bodies: The resurrection involves the transformation of our mortal bodies into glorified bodies, as Jesus' resurrection body was glorified, reflecting Isaiah's hope of bodily resurrection (Strong's Concordance G3345, "μετασχηματίζω" - metaschēmatizō, meaning to transform).

3. Like His Glorious Body: The resurrection body will be like Jesus' glorious body, affirming the continuity and transformation of our physical existence (Strong's Concordance G1391, "δόξα" - doxa, meaning glory).

Comprehensive Commentary

Matthew Henry comments: "Isaiah's prophecy of the dead rising and the earth giving birth to the dead is a powerful anticipation of the resurrection hope fulfilled in Christ. The resurrection of Jesus is the firstfruits, the assurance that all who belong to Him will also be raised to eternal life."

John Calvin, in his Institutes of the Christian Religion, writes: "The prophecy of Isaiah 26:19 is a clear foretelling of the resurrection, a doctrine that is confirmed and realized in the resurrection of Christ. This hope sustains us, knowing that death is not the end, but a passage to eternal life with God."

Theological Implications

1. Assurance of Resurrection: Isaiah 26:19 provides a prophetic foundation for the Christian belief in resurrection, offering assurance that death is not the final word (1 Corinthians 15:54-57).

2. Bodily Resurrection: The emphasis on bodily resurrection in both Isaiah and the New Testament underscores the holistic nature of salvation, involving both body and soul (Philippians 3:20-21).

3. Continuity and Transformation: The resurrection involves both continuity (our bodies) and transformation (glorified bodies), reflecting God's redemptive plan for creation (1 Corinthians 15:42-44).

4. Eternal Life: The promise of eternal life is integral to the resurrection hope, ensuring that believers will enjoy unending fellowship with God (John 11:25-26).

5. Hope in Suffering: The resurrection offers hope in the face of suffering and death, affirming that these are temporary and will be overcome by the power of God (Romans 8:18-23).

Conclusion

Isaiah's hints at the resurrection and eternal life, particularly in Isaiah 26:19, provide a prophetic glimpse into the future hope realized in Jesus Christ. The New Testament teachings on resurrection and eternal life fulfill and expand upon these Old Testament prophecies, affirming the comprehensive and transformative nature of God's redemptive plan.

As we reflect on these promises, we are called to live in the light of the resurrection, embracing the hope and assurance it brings. The correlation between Isaiah's prophecy and New Testament teachings underscores the continuity and fulfillment of God's plan for humanity, offering a profound foundation for faith and hope in eternal life. This chapter has explored Isaiah's prophetic hints and their fulfillment in the New Testament, providing a comprehensive understanding of the resurrection and its theological significance.

Ascension and Reign – Jesus' Ascension to Heaven

The ascension of Jesus Christ to heaven marks a pivotal moment in Christian theology, signifying the completion of His earthly ministry and the beginning of His exalted reign. This event, recorded in Acts 1:9-11, underscores Jesus' divine authority and His eternal kingship. This chapter will explore the ascension of Jesus, examining its biblical accounts, theological implications, and significance for believers. Through an expository study supported by Strong's Concordance and comprehensive commentary, we will delve into the profound meaning of Jesus' ascension and eternal reign.

The Ascension Account in Acts

Acts 1:9-11 (NIV):

"After he said this, he was taken up before their very eyes, and a cloud hid him from their sight. They were looking intently up into the sky as he was going, when suddenly two men dressed in white stood beside them. 'Men of Galilee,' they said, 'why do you stand here looking into the sky? This same Jesus, who has been taken from you into heaven, will come back in the same way you have seen him go into heaven.'"

Analysis

1. Taken Up Before Their Very Eyes: The visible ascension of Jesus is a crucial aspect of this event, affirming His physical departure and return to the Father (Strong's Concordance G1869, "ἐπαίρω" - epairō, meaning to lift up).

2. A Cloud Hid Him: The cloud represents the divine presence, often associated with God's glory and presence in the Scriptures (Strong's Concordance G3507, "νεφέλη" - nephelē, meaning cloud).

3. Two Men in White: The appearance of two angels confirms the divine nature of the ascension and provides reassurance of Jesus' return (Strong's Concordance G32, "ἄγγελος" - angelos, meaning angel).

4. Jesus' Return: The promise of Jesus' return in the same manner emphasizes the certainty of His second coming, providing hope for believers (Strong's Concordance G2064, "ἔρχομαι" - erchomai, meaning to come).

Theological Implications of the Ascension

1. Completion of Earthly Ministry: The ascension signifies the completion of Jesus' earthly mission, culminating in His death, resurrection, and exaltation (Hebrews 10:12).

2. Exaltation and Glory: Jesus' ascension marks His exaltation to the right hand of the Father, a position of authority and glory (Philippians 2:9-11).

3. Intercession for Believers: Jesus ascended to intercede for believers, acting as our high priest and advocate before the Father (Romans 8:34; Hebrews 7:25).

4. Promise of the Holy Spirit: The ascension paved the way for the sending of the Holy Spirit, empowering believers for mission and ministry (John 16:7; Acts 2:33).

5. Preparation of a Place: Jesus ascended to prepare a place for His followers, assuring them of their eternal inheritance (John 14:2-3).

Jesus' Eternal Kingship

Ephesians 1:20-23 (NIV):

"He exerted when he raised Christ from the dead and seated him at his right hand in the heavenly realms, far above all rule and authority, power and dominion, and every name that is invoked, not only in the present age but also in the one to come. And God placed all things under his feet and appointed him to be head over everything for the church, which is his body, the fullness of him who fills everything in every way."

Analysis

1. Seated at the Right Hand: Jesus' position at the right hand of the Father signifies His supreme authority and power (Strong's Concordance G1188, "δεξιός" - dexios, meaning right hand).

2. Far Above All Rule and Authority: Jesus' exaltation places Him above all earthly and spiritual powers, affirming His sovereignty (Strong's Concordance G1849, "ἐξουσία" - exousia, meaning authority).

3. Head Over Everything for the Church: Jesus is appointed as the head of the church, emphasizing His leadership and care for His people (Strong's Concordance G2776, "κεφαλή" - kephalē, meaning head).

The Promise of Jesus' Return

John 14:2-3 (NIV):

"My Father's house has many rooms; if that were not so, would I have told you that I am going there to prepare a place for you? And if I go and prepare a place for you, I will come back and take you to be with me that you also may be where I am."

Analysis

1. Preparing a Place: Jesus' ascension involves preparing an eternal dwelling for believers, assuring them of their future inheritance (Strong's Concordance G2090, "ἑτοιμάζω" - hetoimazō, meaning to prepare).

2. Promise of Return: Jesus' promise to return provides hope and anticipation for believers, affirming the certainty of His second coming (Strong's Concordance G2064, "ἔρχομαι" - erchomai, meaning to come).

Comprehensive Commentary

Matthew Henry comments: "The ascension of Christ is the triumphant conclusion of His earthly ministry, marking His exaltation and enthronement at the right hand of the Father. It provides assurance of His continual intercession and the promise of His return, offering hope and encouragement to believers."

John Calvin, in his Institutes of the Christian Religion, writes: "The ascension of Christ is essential for understanding His exaltation and ongoing ministry. It signifies His victory over death, His sovereign rule, and His role as our advocate. It also assures us of the sending of the Holy Spirit and the preparation of our eternal home."

Theological Significance

1. Completion of Redemptive Work: The ascension signifies the completion of Jesus' redemptive work on earth, affirming His victory over sin and death (Hebrews 10:12).

2. Exaltation and Sovereignty: Jesus' exaltation to the right hand of the Father highlights His sovereignty over all

creation and His authority over the church (Ephesians 1:20-23).

3. Continual Intercession: Jesus' ascension ensures His continual intercession for believers, providing assurance of His ongoing care and advocacy (Romans 8:34).

4. Empowerment by the Holy Spirit: The ascension facilitated the sending of the Holy Spirit, empowering believers for mission and ministry (Acts 1:8).

5. Hope of His Return: The promise of Jesus' return provides hope and anticipation, encouraging believers to live in readiness and faithfulness (Acts 1:11).

Conclusion

The ascension of Jesus Christ is a foundational event in Christian theology, marking the completion of His earthly ministry and the beginning of His exalted reign. Through His ascension, Jesus is exalted to the right hand of the Father, interceding for believers and preparing a place for His followers. This chapter has explored the biblical account of the ascension in Acts 1:9-11, examining its theological implications and significance for believers.

The ascension assures us of Jesus' ongoing ministry, His sovereign rule, and the promise of His return. As we reflect on the ascension, we are called to live in the light of His exaltation, empowered by the Holy Spirit, and filled with hope for His glorious return. This chapter has provided an expository study and comprehensive commentary on the ascension of Jesus, highlighting its profound theological significance and enduring relevance for the Christian faith.

Fulfillment of Isaiah's Prophecy of an Everlasting Kingdom

Isaiah 9:7 contains a powerful prophecy about the Messiah's everlasting kingdom. This verse foretells a ruler whose government and peace will have no end, seated on David's throne and upheld with justice and righteousness. This chapter will explore the fulfillment of Isaiah's prophecy in the person and reign of Jesus Christ, examining how the New Testament confirms this fulfillment and the theological implications of an everlasting kingdom. Through an expository study supported by Strong's Concordance and comprehensive commentary, we will uncover the deep significance of Isaiah 9:7.

Isaiah's Prophecy of an Everlasting Kingdom

Isaiah 9:7 (NIV):

"Of the greatness of his government and peace there will be no end. He will reign on David's throne and over his kingdom, establishing and upholding it with justice and righteousness from that time on and forever. The zeal of the Lord Almighty will accomplish this."

Analysis

1. "Of the greatness of his government and peace there will be no end": This indicates an eternal and expanding reign characterized by peace (Strong's Concordance H4768, "מַרְבֵּה" - marbeh, meaning increase or greatness).

2. "He will reign on David's throne and over his kingdom": This identifies the Messiah as a descendant of David, fulfilling the Davidic covenant (Strong's Concordance H4428, "מֶלֶךְ" - melek, meaning king).

3. "Establishing and upholding it with justice and righteousness": The Messiah's reign will be marked by divine justice and righteousness (Strong's Concordance H4941, "מִשְׁפָּט" - mishpat, meaning judgment or justice; H6666, "צְדָקָה" - tsedaqah, meaning righteousness).

4. "From that time on and forever": The eternal nature of the kingdom is emphasized, indicating an unending reign (Strong's Concordance H5703, "עַד" - ad, meaning forever or everlasting).

5. "The zeal of the Lord Almighty will accomplish this": The fulfillment of this prophecy is guaranteed by God's passionate commitment (Strong's Concordance H7068, "קִנְאָה" - qinah, meaning zeal or ardor).

Fulfillment in the New Testament

The New Testament writers explicitly connect the life and reign of Jesus Christ with the fulfillment of Isaiah's prophecy of an everlasting kingdom.

Jesus' Davidic Lineage

Luke 1:32-33 (NIV):

"He will be great and will be called the Son of the Most High. The Lord God will give him the throne of his father David, and he will reign over Jacob's descendants forever; his kingdom will never end."

Analysis

1. Son of the Most High: Jesus is identified as the divine Son of God, fulfilling the messianic expectation (Strong's Concordance G5310, "ὕψιστος" - hypsistos, meaning highest).

2. Throne of David: Jesus' reign on David's throne fulfills the Davidic covenant and Isaiah's prophecy (Strong's Concordance G2362, "θρόνος" - thronos, meaning throne).

3. Reign Over Jacob's Descendants Forever: The eternal nature of Jesus' reign is emphasized, affirming the everlasting kingdom (Strong's Concordance G165, "αἰών" - aiōn, meaning age or forever).

Jesus' Eternal Kingship

Revelation 11:15 (NIV):

"The seventh angel sounded his trumpet, and there were loud voices in heaven, which said: 'The kingdom of the world has become the kingdom of our Lord and of his Messiah, and he will reign for ever and ever.'"

Analysis

1. Kingdom of the World: The transformation of the world's kingdoms into the kingdom of Christ signifies His ultimate authority (Strong's Concordance G932, "βασιλεία" - basileia, meaning kingdom).

2. Reign for Ever and Ever: The eternal reign of Christ is declared, fulfilling Isaiah's prophecy of an everlasting kingdom (Strong's Concordance G165, "αἰών" - aiōn, meaning age or forever).

The Justice and Righteousness of Jesus' Reign

Romans 3:21-22 (NIV):

"But now apart from the law the righteousness of God has been made known, to which the Law and the Prophets testify. This righteousness is given through faith in Jesus Christ to all who believe. There is no difference between Jew and Gentile."

Analysis

1. Righteousness of God: Jesus reveals God's righteousness, fulfilling the messianic expectation of a just

and righteous reign (Strong's Concordance G1343, "δικαιοσύνη" - dikaiosynē, meaning righteousness).

2. Testimony of the Law and the Prophets: Isaiah's prophecy is part of this testimony, pointing to the fulfillment in Christ (Strong's Concordance G3142, "μαρτυρία" - martyria, meaning testimony).

3. Given Through Faith in Jesus: The righteousness of Christ's kingdom is accessible to all who believe, emphasizing its universal scope (Strong's Concordance G4100, "πιστεύω" - pisteuō, meaning to believe).

The Eternal Nature of Jesus' Reign

Hebrews 1:8 (NIV):

"But about the Son he says, 'Your throne, O God, will last for ever and ever; a scepter of justice will be the scepter of your kingdom.'"

Analysis

1. Your Throne, O God: Jesus is addressed as God, affirming His divine kingship (Strong's Concordance G2316, "θεός" - theos, meaning God).

2. Last for Ever and Ever: The eternal nature of Jesus' reign is declared, in line with Isaiah's prophecy (Strong's Concordance G165, "αἰών" - aiōn, meaning age or forever).

3. Scepter of Justice: The reign of Jesus is characterized by justice, fulfilling the messianic expectation of a just ruler (Strong's Concordance G2118, "ῥάβδος" - rhabdos, meaning rod or scepter).

Comprehensive Commentary

Matthew Henry comments: "Isaiah's prophecy of an everlasting kingdom finds its fulfillment in the person and reign of Jesus Christ. His kingdom is established with justice and righteousness, upheld by the zeal of the Lord. The New Testament confirms this fulfillment, showing Jesus as the eternal king who reigns on David's throne forever."

John Calvin, in his Institutes of the Christian Religion, writes: "The prophecy of Isaiah 9:7 is a clear testimony to the eternal kingship of Christ. The New Testament reveals the fulfillment of this promise in the exaltation of Jesus, who reigns with justice and righteousness. His kingdom is not of this world but is an everlasting dominion that brings peace and salvation to all who believe."

Theological Implications

1. Eternal Kingship: Jesus' eternal kingship fulfills the prophetic hope of an everlasting kingdom, providing assurance of His unending reign (Revelation 11:15).

2. Justice and Righteousness: The reign of Jesus is marked by divine justice and righteousness, reflecting the

character of God and fulfilling the messianic expectations (Romans 3:21-22).

3. Universal Scope: The kingdom of Jesus is inclusive, extending to all who believe, regardless of ethnicity or background (Galatians 3:28).

4. Divine Authority: Jesus' reign on David's throne signifies His divine authority and fulfillment of the Davidic covenant, affirming His rightful place as the Messiah (Luke 1:32-33).

5. Hope and Assurance: The fulfillment of Isaiah's prophecy in Jesus provides believers with hope and assurance of God's sovereign plan and the ultimate victory of His kingdom (Hebrews 1:8).

Conclusion

Isaiah's prophecy of an everlasting kingdom, as recorded in Isaiah 9:7, finds its fulfillment in the person and reign of Jesus Christ. The New Testament writers explicitly connect Jesus' life, death, resurrection, and exaltation with this prophecy, affirming His eternal kingship and divine authority. The theological implications of this fulfillment are profound, encompassing the eternal nature of Jesus' reign, the justice and righteousness of His kingdom, and the universal scope of His rule.

As we reflect on the fulfillment of Isaiah's prophecy, we are called to recognize and submit to the reign of Jesus, living in the light of His eternal kingdom. This chapter has explored the profound connections between Isaiah's prophecy and New Testament teachings, offering a comprehensive understanding of the everlasting kingdom promised and fulfilled in Christ.

CHAPTER 06

THE IMPACT OF JESUS' TEACHING TODAY – LIVING THE BEATITUDES

The Beatitudes, found in Matthew 5:3-12, are among the most profound teachings of Jesus, forming the opening of His Sermon on the Mount. These statements outline the attitudes and behaviors that characterize the blessed life in God's kingdom. This chapter will explore the practical application of the Beatitudes in modern life, examining each Beatitude in detail and considering how these teachings can transform our daily living. Through an expository study supported by Strong's Concordance and comprehensive commentary, we will uncover the enduring relevance and impact of the Beatitudes.

The Beatitudes in Matthew

Matthew 5:3-12 (NIV):

"Blessed are the poor in spirit, for theirs is the kingdom of heaven.

Blessed are those who mourn, for they will be comforted.

Blessed are the meek, for they will inherit the earth.

Blessed are those who hunger and thirst for righteousness, for they will be filled.

Blessed are the merciful, for they will be shown mercy.

Blessed are the pure in heart, for they will see God.

Blessed are the peacemakers, for they will be called children of God.

Blessed are those who are persecuted because of righteousness, for theirs is the kingdom of heaven.

Blessed are you when people insult you, persecute you and falsely say all kinds of evil against you because of me. Rejoice and be glad, because great is your reward in heaven, for in the same way they persecuted the prophets who were before you."

Expository Study and Practical Application

1. Blessed are the Poor in Spirit

Matthew 5:3: "Blessed are the poor in spirit, for theirs is the kingdom of heaven."

Analysis:

- Poor in Spirit: Recognizing one's spiritual poverty and dependence on God (Strong's Concordance G4434, "πτωχός" - ptōchos, meaning poor or destitute).

- Kingdom of Heaven: The reward for humility and dependence on God is participation in His kingdom (Strong's Concordance G932, "βασιλεία" - basileia, meaning kingdom).

Application:

Living in humility and recognizing our need for God is foundational for the Christian life. In modern contexts, this means acknowledging our limitations and relying on God's strength and grace in all circumstances. It involves a heart attitude that seeks God's guidance and remains open to His leading.

2. Blessed are Those Who Mourn

Matthew 5:4: "Blessed are those who mourn, for they will be comforted."

Analysis:

- Mourn: Experiencing sorrow, particularly over sin and suffering in the world (Strong's Concordance G3996, "πενθέω" - pentheō, meaning to mourn).

- Comforted: The promise of divine comfort and consolation (Strong's Concordance G3870, "παρακαλέω" - parakaleō, meaning to comfort or encourage).

Application:

Mourning over sin and brokenness leads to repentance and a deeper reliance on God. In modern life, this involves being sensitive to the suffering around us, engaging in acts of compassion, and seeking justice. It also means finding comfort in God's presence and promises during times of personal loss and grief.

3. Blessed are the Meek

Matthew 5:5: "Blessed are the meek, for they will inherit the earth."

Analysis:

- Meek: Demonstrating gentleness and humility (Strong's Concordance G4239, "πραΰς" - praus, meaning meek or gentle).

- Inherit the Earth: The promise of a future reward for those who live with humility (Strong's Concordance G2816, "κληρονομέω" - klēronomeō, meaning to inherit).

Application:

Meekness involves strength under control and a gentle spirit. In modern contexts, this means treating others with kindness, avoiding retaliation, and practicing patience. It is about leading by example and showing humility in relationships and leadership.

4. Blessed are Those Who Hunger and Thirst for Righteousness

Matthew 5:6: "Blessed are those who hunger and thirst for righteousness, for they will be filled."

Analysis:

- Hunger and Thirst: Intense desire and longing for righteousness (Strong's Concordance G3983, "πεινάω" - peinaō, meaning to hunger; G1372, "διψάω" - dipsaō, meaning to thirst).

- Righteousness: Living in a way that is pleasing to God, characterized by justice and moral integrity (Strong's Concordance G1343, "δικαιοσύνη" - dikaiosynē, meaning righteousness).

Application:

Pursuing righteousness involves seeking God's will and striving for moral excellence. In modern life, this means advocating for justice, living ethically, and aligning our actions with God's standards. It requires a commitment to personal holiness and social justice.

5. Blessed are the Merciful

Matthew 5:7: "Blessed are the merciful, for they will be shown mercy."

Analysis:

- Merciful: Showing compassion and forgiveness to others (Strong's Concordance G1655, "ἐλεήμων" - eleēmōn, meaning merciful).

- Shown Mercy: The reciprocal nature of mercy, receiving divine mercy in return (Strong's Concordance G1653, "ἐλεέω" - eleeō, meaning to show mercy).

Application:

Practicing mercy involves forgiving others, showing kindness, and offering help to those in need. In modern contexts, this means being empathetic and understanding, extending grace, and engaging in acts of charity. It fosters a community of support and compassion.

6. Blessed are the Pure in Heart

Matthew 5:8: "Blessed are the pure in heart, for they will see God."

Analysis:

- Pure in Heart: Having a heart that is free from sin and deceit, characterized by sincerity and holiness (Strong's Concordance G2513, "καθαρός" - katharos, meaning pure).

- See God: The promise of intimate fellowship with God (Strong's Concordance G3700, "ὁράω" - horaō, meaning to see or perceive).

Application:

Purity of heart involves maintaining integrity and holiness in thoughts, motives, and actions. In modern life, this means striving for moral purity, avoiding corruption, and living transparently. It fosters a deeper relationship with God and clarity in spiritual vision.

7. Blessed are the Peacemakers

Matthew 5:9: "Blessed are the peacemakers, for they will be called children of God."

Analysis:

- Peacemakers: Actively working to reconcile and create harmony (Strong's Concordance G1518, "εἰρηνοποιός" - eirēnopoios, meaning peacemaker).

- Children of God: Identifying with God's family through the pursuit of peace (Strong's Concordance G5207, "υἱός" - huios, meaning son or child).

Application:

Being a peacemaker involves resolving conflicts, promoting reconciliation, and fostering unity. In modern contexts, this means advocating for peace in personal relationships, communities, and global affairs. It involves being a mediator and a voice for harmony.

8. Blessed are Those Who are Persecuted for Righteousness

Matthew 5:10: "Blessed are those who are persecuted because of righteousness, for theirs is the kingdom of heaven."

Analysis:

- Persecuted for Righteousness: Suffering for doing what is right and standing for God's principles (Strong's Concordance G1377, "διώκω" - diōkō, meaning to persecute).

- Kingdom of Heaven: The assurance of God's reign and reward for enduring persecution (Strong's Concordance G932, "βασιλεία" - basileia, meaning kingdom).

Application:

Enduring persecution for righteousness involves standing firm in faith despite opposition and hardship. In modern life, this means maintaining integrity, defending truth, and facing societal pressures with courage. It brings the assurance of God's presence and future reward.

9. Blessed are You When People Insult You

Matthew 5:11-12: "Blessed are you when people insult you, persecute you and falsely say all kinds of evil against you because of me. Rejoice and be glad, because great is your reward in heaven, for in the same way they persecuted the prophets who were before you."

Analysis:

- Insult and Persecution: Experiencing verbal and physical abuse for the sake of Christ (Strong's Concordance G3679, "ὀνειδίζω" - oneidizō, meaning to insult).

- Rejoice and Be Glad: The call to respond with joy in the face of persecution, recognizing the eternal reward (Strong's Concordance G5463, "χαίρω" - chairō, meaning to rejoice).

Application:

Facing insults and persecution with joy involves recognizing the eternal significance of suffering for Christ. In modern contexts, this means remaining steadfast in faith, finding joy in trials, and focusing on the eternal reward. It encourages perseverance and a Christ-like response to adversity.

Comprehensive Commentary

Matthew Henry comments: "The Beatitudes are a comprehensive summary of the

Christian character, outlining the attitudes and behaviors that are blessed by God. They call believers to live in humility, righteousness, mercy, purity, and peace, even in the face of persecution. The promises attached to each Beatitude provide assurance of God's favor and the ultimate reward of eternal life."

John Calvin, in his Institutes of the Christian Religion, writes: "The Beatitudes set forth the virtues that are pleasing to God and the blessings that accompany them. They are not merely ethical guidelines but profound spiritual truths that reveal the nature of the kingdom of God. Living the Beatitudes is a response to God's grace and a manifestation of the transformative power of the gospel."

Theological Implications

1. Kingdom Living: The Beatitudes describe the lifestyle of those who belong to the kingdom of God, characterized by humility, righteousness, and mercy (Matthew 5:3-12).

2. Eternal Perspective: The promises of the Beatitudes shift our focus from temporary suffering to eternal reward, encouraging perseverance and faithfulness (2 Corinthians 4:17-18).

3. Transformative Power: Living the Beatitudes demonstrates the transformative power of the gospel, as believers embody the values of the kingdom in their daily lives (Romans 12:1-2).

4. Community and Witness: The Beatitudes foster a sense of community among believers and serve as a powerful witness to the world of God's love and grace (John 13:34-35).

5. Spiritual Growth: Practicing the Beatitudes leads to spiritual growth and maturity, as believers develop Christ-like character and deepen their relationship with God (Galatians 5:22-23).

Conclusion

The Beatitudes, as taught by Jesus in the Sermon on the Mount, provide a blueprint for living a blessed and fulfilled life in God's kingdom. Each Beatitude contains a profound truth and a promise, offering guidance and encouragement for believers. By living the Beatitudes, we align our lives with God's values, experience His blessings, and become a powerful witness to His transforming grace.

This chapter has explored the practical application of the Beatitudes in modern life, offering an expository study and comprehensive commentary on each statement. As we embrace these teachings, we are called to live in humility, righteousness, mercy, purity, and peace, reflecting the character of Christ and advancing His kingdom in our world.

How Jesus' Teachings Continue to Influence Christian Ethics and Behavior

The teachings of Jesus Christ have profoundly shaped Christian ethics and behavior for centuries. His words and actions provide a foundation for moral decision-making, personal conduct, and societal norms within the Christian community. This chapter will explore how Jesus' teachings continue to influence Christian ethics and behavior, examining key principles and their practical applications in modern life. Through an expository study supported by Strong's Concordance and comprehensive commentary, we will uncover the enduring relevance of Jesus' teachings for ethical living and behavior.

The Greatest Commandment

Matthew 22:37-40 (NIV):

"Jesus replied: 'Love the Lord your God with all your heart and with all your soul and with all your mind.' This is the first and greatest commandment. And the second is like it: 'Love your neighbor as yourself.' All the Law and the Prophets hang on these two commandments."

Analysis

1. Love God: The command to love God with all one's heart, soul, and mind emphasizes total devotion and commitment to God (Strong's Concordance G25, "ἀγαπάω" - agapaō, meaning to love).

2. Love Your Neighbor: Loving one's neighbor as oneself highlights the importance of empathy, compassion, and selflessness in relationships (Strong's Concordance G25, "ἀγαπάω" - agapaō, meaning to love).

3. Foundation of the Law: These two commandments summarize the ethical demands of the entire Old Testament, reflecting the holistic nature of Jesus' ethical teachings (Strong's Concordance G3551, "νόμος" - nomos, meaning law).

Application:

The Greatest Commandment serves as the foundation for Christian ethics. In modern life, this involves prioritizing our relationship with God through worship, prayer, and obedience. Loving our neighbor translates into acts of kindness, justice, and service, fostering a community of mutual care and respect.

The Golden Rule

Matthew 7:12 (NIV):

"So in everything, do to others what you would have them do to you, for this sums up the Law and the Prophets."

Analysis

1. Do to Others: The Golden Rule calls for proactive and positive treatment of others, emphasizing reciprocity and empathy (Strong's Concordance G4160, "ποιέω" - poieō, meaning to do).

2. Summary of the Law: This principle encapsulates the ethical teachings of the Law and the Prophets,

highlighting its comprehensive nature (Strong's Concordance G3551, "νόμος" - nomos, meaning law).

Application:

The Golden Rule influences Christian behavior by encouraging believers to treat others with the same respect and consideration they desire. In modern contexts, this involves fairness, honesty, and integrity in personal and professional relationships, promoting a culture of respect and mutual benefit.

The Sermon on the Mount

The Sermon on the Mount (Matthew 5-7) contains key ethical teachings that continue to shape Christian behavior.

The Beatitudes

Matthew 5:3-12 (NIV):

The Beatitudes outline the attitudes and behaviors that characterize the blessed life in God's kingdom.

Application:

Living the Beatitudes involves humility, compassion, meekness, righteousness, mercy, purity, peace, and perseverance. These values influence personal conduct, social interactions, and community life, fostering a culture of grace and integrity.

Salt and Light

Matthew 5:13-16 (NIV):

"You are the salt of the earth. But if the salt loses its saltiness, how can it be made salty again? It is no longer good for anything, except to be thrown out and trampled underfoot. You are the light of the world. A town built on a hill cannot be hidden. Neither do people light a lamp and put it under a bowl. Instead they put it on its stand, and it gives light to everyone in the house. In the same way, let your light shine before others, that they may see your good deeds and glorify your Father in heaven."

Analysis

1. Salt of the Earth: Christians are called to preserve and enhance the moral fabric of society, reflecting God's holiness (Strong's Concordance G217, "ἅλας" - halas, meaning salt).

2. Light of the World: Believers are to be visible examples of God's truth and love, illuminating the world with their good deeds (Strong's Concordance G5457, "φῶς" - phōs, meaning light).

Application:

Being salt and light involves living out Christian values in a way that positively impacts society. This means promoting moral integrity, justice, and compassion, and being a visible witness to God's love through acts of service and advocacy for the marginalized.

Love for Enemies

Matthew 5:43-45 (NIV):

"You have heard that it was said, 'Love your neighbor and hate your enemy.' But I tell you, love your enemies and pray for those who persecute you, that you may be children of your Father in heaven."

Analysis

1. Love Your Enemies: Jesus' radical command to love enemies challenges conventional attitudes and calls for transformative love (Strong's Concordance G25, "ἀγαπάω" - agapaō, meaning to love).

2. Pray for Persecutors: Praying for those who persecute us fosters a spirit of forgiveness and reconciliation (Strong's Concordance G4336, "προσεύχομαι" - proseuchomai, meaning to pray).

Application:

Loving enemies involves extending grace and forgiveness to those who oppose or harm us. In modern life, this means seeking reconciliation, refusing to retaliate, and promoting peace and understanding in the face of conflict and hostility.

The Parable of the Good Samaritan

Luke 10:25-37 (NIV):

The Parable of the Good Samaritan highlights the importance of compassion and action in ethical living.

Analysis

1. Compassion for Others: The Samaritan's compassion for the injured man exemplifies selfless love and care for others (Strong's Concordance G4697, "σπλαγχνίζομαι" - splagchnizomai, meaning to have compassion).

2. Action in Love: The Samaritan's actions demonstrate that true love involves practical help and sacrifice (Strong's Concordance G4160, "ποιέω" - poieō, meaning to do).

Application:

Living out the Good Samaritan's example involves showing compassion and taking action to help those in need. In modern contexts, this means engaging in social justice, humanitarian efforts, and everyday acts of kindness, reflecting God's love through tangible actions.

Forgiveness and Reconciliation

Matthew 18:21-22 (NIV):

"Then Peter came to Jesus and asked, 'Lord, how many times shall I forgive my brother or sister who sins against me? Up to seven times?' Jesus answered, 'I tell you, not seven times, but seventy-seven times.'"

Analysis

1. Unlimited Forgiveness: Jesus teaches that forgiveness should be limitless, reflecting God's grace (Strong's Concordance G863, "ἀφίημι" - aphiēmi, meaning to forgive).

2. Spirit of Reconciliation: Forgiveness fosters reconciliation and restores relationships, embodying the kingdom values of grace and mercy (Strong's Concordance G2644, "καταλλάσσω" - katallassō, meaning to reconcile).

Application:

Practicing forgiveness involves letting go of grudges and extending grace to others. In modern life, this means resolving conflicts, seeking to mend broken relationships, and promoting a culture of forgiveness and reconciliation in families, communities, and workplaces.

Theological Implications

1. Love and Compassion: Jesus' teachings emphasize love and compassion as central to Christian ethics, guiding believers in their relationships with God and others (Matthew 22:37-40).

2. Holistic Righteousness: Christian ethics encompass both personal holiness and social justice, reflecting the comprehensive nature of Jesus' moral teachings (Matthew 5-7).

3. Transformative Power: Living according to Jesus' teachings transforms individuals and communities, fostering a culture of grace, mercy, and justice (Romans 12:1-2).

4. Kingdom Values: Jesus' teachings align with the values of God's kingdom, promoting humility, mercy, purity, and peace as foundational for ethical living (Matthew 5:3-12).

5. Eternal Perspective: Jesus' ethical teachings encourage believers to live with an eternal perspective, focusing on the ultimate reward and fulfillment in God's kingdom (Matthew 6:19-21).

Comprehensive Commentary

Matthew Henry comments: "The teachings of Jesus provide a clear and compelling guide for Christian ethics, emphasizing love, compassion, and righteousness. They call believers to a higher standard of living that reflects the values of God's kingdom and transforms society."

John Calvin, in his Institutes of the Christian Religion, writes: "The ethical teachings of Christ are not merely rules to follow but are expressions of the grace and truth that come from God. They reveal the character of God and the way of life that pleases Him, guiding believers in their daily conduct and relationships."

Conclusion

The teachings of Jesus continue to profoundly influence Christian ethics and behavior, providing a timeless foundation for moral decision-making and personal conduct. From the Greatest Commandment to the Golden Rule, from the Beatitudes to the call to love enemies, Jesus' words challenge and inspire believers to live lives marked by love, compassion, and righteousness.

This chapter has explored the practical application of Jesus' teachings, offering an expository study and comprehensive commentary on how these teachings shape modern Christian ethics. As we embrace and live out these teachings, we reflect the values of God's kingdom, fostering a culture of grace, mercy, and justice in our world.

The Great Commission – The Command to Spread the Gospel

The Great Commission, recorded in Matthew 28:19-20, is one of the most significant and enduring commands given by Jesus Christ to His disciples. This mandate to spread the gospel to all nations forms the foundation of Christian mission and evangelism. This chapter will explore the Great Commission in detail, examining its biblical context, theological implications, and practical applications for modern believers. Through an expository study supported by Strong's Concordance and comprehensive commentary, we will uncover the profound significance of this command and its impact on the global mission of the Church.

The Great Commission in Matthew

Matthew 28:19-20 (NIV):

"Therefore go and make disciples of all nations, baptizing them in the name of the Father and of the Son and of the Holy Spirit, and teaching them to obey everything I have commanded you. And surely I am with you always, to the very end of the age."

Analysis

1. "Therefore go": The imperative "go" signifies active movement and intentional effort to reach others (Strong's Concordance G4198, "πορεύομαι" - poreuomai, meaning to go or proceed).

2. "Make disciples": The primary task is to make disciples, indicating a process of teaching and nurturing believers (Strong's Concordance G3100, "μαθητεύω" - mathēteuō, meaning to make disciples or instruct).

3. "Of all nations": The scope of the mission is global, encompassing all ethnic and cultural groups (Strong's Concordance G1484, "ἔθνος" - ethnos, meaning nations or peoples).

4. "Baptizing them": Baptism is an essential element of discipleship, symbolizing identification with Christ and

initiation into the Christian community (Strong's Concordance G907, "βαπτίζω" - baptizō, meaning to baptize).

5. "In the name of the Father and of the Son and of the Holy Spirit": This Trinitarian formula emphasizes the unity and distinct roles of the Godhead in the process of salvation and discipleship (Strong's Concordance G3686, "ὄνομα" - onoma, meaning name).

6. "Teaching them to obey everything I have commanded you": Discipleship involves ongoing instruction and adherence to Jesus' teachings (Strong's Concordance G1321, "διδάσκω" - didaskō, meaning to teach).

7. "Surely I am with you always": The promise of Jesus' continual presence provides assurance and encouragement for the mission (Strong's Concordance G3956, "πᾶς" - pas, meaning all or every).

8. "To the very end of the age": The mission has an eschatological dimension, continuing until the culmination of history (Strong's Concordance G165, "αἰών" - aiōn, meaning age or era).

Theological Implications of the Great Commission

1. Universal Mission: The command to make disciples of all nations underscores the universal scope of the gospel, transcending cultural and geographical boundaries (Acts 1:8).

2. Baptism and Trinitarian Theology: The inclusion of baptism in the name of the Father, Son, and Holy Spirit highlights the Trinitarian nature of Christian faith and the integral role of the Trinity in salvation (Romans 6:3-4).

3. Teaching and Obedience: Discipleship involves comprehensive teaching and a call to obedience, emphasizing the importance of sound doctrine and ethical living (John 14:15).

4. Presence of Christ: The promise of Jesus' presence assures believers of divine support and guidance in their mission, reinforcing the continuity of Christ's ministry through the Church (Matthew 18:20).

5. Eschatological Hope: The mission is carried out with an awareness of the end times, motivating believers to remain steadfast and diligent in spreading the gospel (2 Peter 3:9-13).

Practical Applications of the Great Commission

Evangelism

Mark 16:15 (NIV):

"He said to them, 'Go into all the world and preach the gospel to all creation.'"

Application:

Evangelism involves actively sharing the good news of Jesus Christ with others. In modern contexts, this can be done through personal conversations, public preaching, media outreach, and social media platforms. It requires a commitment to communicate the message of salvation clearly and compassionately.

Discipleship

2 Timothy 2:2 (NIV):

"And the things you have heard me say in the presence of many witnesses entrust to reliable people who will also be qualified to teach others."

Application:

Discipleship is the process of nurturing new believers and helping them grow in their faith. This involves regular Bible study, prayer, mentoring, and providing opportunities for service. Effective discipleship programs focus on building mature, equipped, and reproducing followers of Christ.

Baptism

Romans 6:3-4 (NIV):

"Or don't you know that all of us who were baptized into Christ Jesus were baptized into his death? We were therefore buried with him through baptism into death in order that, just as Christ was raised from the dead through the glory of the Father, we too may live a new life."

Application:

Baptism serves as a public declaration of faith and identification with the death and resurrection of Jesus. Churches should provide clear teachings on the significance of baptism and ensure that new believers have the opportunity to be baptized as part of their discipleship journey.

Teaching and Obedience

John 14:15 (NIV):

"If you love me, keep my commands."

Application:

Teaching the commands of Jesus involves providing sound biblical instruction and encouraging practical application in everyday life. This can be achieved through sermons, Bible studies, small groups, and personal mentorship. Emphasizing obedience to Jesus' teachings helps believers live out their faith authentically.

Assurance of Christ's Presence

Hebrews 13:5-6 (NIV):

"Keep your lives free from the love of money and be content with what you have, because God has said, 'Never will I leave you; never will I forsake you.' So we say with confidence, 'The Lord is my helper; I will not be afraid. What can mere mortals do to me?'"

Application:

Believers are encouraged by the promise of Jesus' continual presence. This assurance should embolden them to undertake the Great Commission with confidence, knowing that Christ is with them every step of the way. This presence is experienced through prayer, the Holy Spirit, and the support of the Christian community.

Comprehensive Commentary

Matthew Henry comments: "The Great Commission is the grand charter of the Church. It is a comprehensive and enduring command that encompasses evangelism, discipleship, and teaching. The promise of Christ's presence provides comfort and encouragement, assuring believers that they do not undertake this mission alone."

John Calvin, in his Institutes of the Christian Religion, writes: "The command to make disciples of all nations is a divine mandate that reflects God's heart for the world. It calls believers to an active and intentional engagement in spreading the gospel, baptizing new converts, and teaching them to obey Christ's commands. This mission is carried out with the assurance of Christ's continual presence and support."

Theological Significance

1. Global Mission: The Great Commission emphasizes the global nature of the Christian mission, calling believers to reach all people with the gospel (Matthew 28:19).

2. Trinitarian Baptism: The Trinitarian formula for baptism reflects the unity and distinct roles of the Father, Son, and Holy Spirit in the work of salvation (Matthew 28:19).

3. Discipleship and Teaching: The command to teach obedience to Jesus' commands highlights the importance of sound doctrine and ethical living in the Christian life (Matthew 28:20).

4. Presence of Christ: The promise of Jesus' presence assures believers of divine support and guidance, reinforcing the continuity of Christ's ministry through the Church (Matthew 28:20).

5. Eschatological Dimension: The mission is carried out with an awareness of the end times, motivating believers to remain steadfast and diligent in spreading the gospel (Matthew 28:20).

Conclusion

The Great Commission, as recorded in Matthew 28:19-20, is a foundational command that continues to shape the mission and activities of the Church. It calls believers to make disciples of all nations, baptizing them and teaching them to obey Jesus' commands, with the assurance of His continual presence.

This chapter has explored the Great Commission in detail, offering an expository study and comprehensive commentary on its biblical context, theological implications, and practical applications. As we embrace and fulfill this mandate, we participate in God's redemptive plan for the world, spreading the gospel and advancing His kingdom until the very end of the age.

The Global Impact of Jesus' Teachings and the Fulfillment of Isaiah's Vision for the Nations

The teachings of Jesus Christ have had a profound and lasting impact on individuals, communities, and nations around the world. This global influence is seen as the fulfillment of Isaiah's vision for the nations, particularly as articulated in Isaiah 49:6. This chapter will explore the global impact of Jesus' teachings and how they fulfill Isaiah's prophetic vision. Through an expository study supported by Strong's Concordance and comprehensive commentary, we will examine the significance of Jesus' teachings in shaping the moral, cultural, and spiritual landscape of the world.

Isaiah's Vision for the Nations

Isaiah 49:6 (NIV):

"He says: 'It is too small a thing for you to be my servant to restore the tribes of Jacob and bring back those of Israel I have kept. I will also make you a light for the Gentiles, that my salvation may reach to the ends of the earth.'"

Analysis

1. "Too small a thing": The mission of the Servant of the Lord is not limited to Israel but extends to the entire world (Strong's Concordance H7043, "קָלַל" - qalal, meaning to be small or insignificant).

2. "Restore the tribes of Jacob": The Servant's role includes the restoration of Israel (Strong's Concordance H7725, "שׁוּב" - shuwb, meaning to return or restore).

3. "Light for the Gentiles": The Servant is also a light for the Gentiles, indicating a universal mission (Strong's Concordance H1471, "גּוֹי" - goy, meaning nation or people).

4. "My salvation may reach to the ends of the earth": The ultimate goal is the spread of God's salvation to all nations (Strong's Concordance H3444, "יְשׁוּעָה" - yĕshuw`ah, meaning salvation).

Fulfillment in the Teachings of Jesus

Jesus' teachings and the Great Commission embody the fulfillment of Isaiah's vision, extending the message of salvation to all nations.

The Great Commission

Matthew 28:19-20 (NIV):

"Therefore go and make disciples of all nations, baptizing them in the name of the Father and of the Son and of the Holy Spirit, and teaching them to obey everything I have commanded you. And surely I am with you always, to the very end of the age."

Analysis:

- "All nations": The command to make disciples of all nations aligns with Isaiah's vision of salvation reaching the ends of the earth (Strong's Concordance G1484, "ἔθνος" - ethnos, meaning nations or peoples).

- "Teaching them to obey": Jesus' teachings are to be disseminated globally, ensuring that all nations learn and adhere to His commands (Strong's Concordance G1321, "διδάσκω" - didaskō, meaning to teach).

Application:

The Great Commission underscores the global mission of the Church. Modern believers are called to participate in this mission through evangelism, discipleship, and teaching, ensuring that the gospel reaches every corner of the world.

Light to the Gentiles

John 8:12 (NIV):

"When Jesus spoke again to the people, he said, 'I am the light of the world. Whoever follows me will never walk in darkness, but will have the light of life.'"

Analysis:

- "Light of the world": Jesus identifies Himself as the light, fulfilling the role prophesied by Isaiah (Strong's Concordance G5457, "φῶς" - phōs, meaning light).

- "Light of life": Following Jesus brings enlightenment and life, fulfilling the prophecy of salvation reaching the Gentiles (Strong's Concordance G2222, "ζωή" - zōē, meaning life).

Application:

As the light of the world, Jesus illuminates the path to salvation for all people. Believers are called to reflect this light, sharing the message of Jesus with others and guiding them out of spiritual darkness.

Global Impact of Jesus' Teachings

Transformation of Societies

Galatians 3:28 (NIV):

"There is neither Jew nor Gentile, neither slave nor free, nor is there male and female, for you are all one in Christ Jesus."

Analysis:

- "Neither Jew nor Gentile": Jesus' teachings break down ethnic and cultural barriers, promoting unity and equality (Strong's Concordance G2453, "Ἰουδαῖος" - Ioudaios, meaning Jew; G1672, "Ἕλλην" - Hellēn, meaning Greek or Gentile)

- "All one in Christ Jesus": The message of unity in Christ transcends social divisions, creating a new community of believers (Strong's Concordance G1520, "εἷς" - heis, meaning one).

Application:

Jesus' teachings have transformed societies by promoting values of equality, justice, and unity. In modern contexts, this involves advocating for social justice, challenging discrimination, and fostering inclusive communities that reflect the unity of the body of Christ.

Ethical and Moral Standards

Matthew 5:16 (NIV):

"In the same way, let your light shine before others, that they may see your good deeds and glorify your Father in heaven."

Analysis:

- "Let your light shine": Believers are called to exemplify ethical and moral behavior, reflecting the teachings of Jesus (Strong's Concordance G2989, "λάμπω" - lampō, meaning to shine).

- "Good deeds": The emphasis on good deeds underscores the importance of living out Christian ethics in practical ways (Strong's Concordance G2041, "ἔργον" - ergon, meaning work or deed).

Application:

Jesus' ethical teachings continue to influence personal and communal behavior, promoting honesty, integrity, and compassion. Modern believers are called to live out these values in their daily lives, serving as examples of Christ-like conduct in a diverse world.

Expansion of the Church

Acts 1:8 (NIV):

"But you will receive power when the Holy Spirit comes on you; and you will be my witnesses in Jerusalem, and in all Judea and Samaria, and to the ends of the earth."

Analysis:

- "You will be my witnesses": The disciples are commissioned to testify about Jesus, spreading the gospel message globally (Strong's Concordance G3144, "μάρτυς" - martys, meaning witness).

- "Ends of the earth": The scope of the mission extends to the entire world, fulfilling Isaiah's vision of global salvation (Strong's Concordance G1093, "γῆ" - gē, meaning earth or land).

Application:

The rapid expansion of the Church in the first century and beyond demonstrates the fulfillment of Jesus' command and Isaiah's vision. Modern believers continue this mission through church planting, missions, and evangelistic efforts, ensuring that the gospel reaches every nation.

Theological Implications

1. Universal Salvation: The global mission of Jesus' teachings fulfills Isaiah's vision of salvation reaching all nations, affirming the inclusivity of the gospel (Isaiah 49:6).

2. Role of the Church: The Church is tasked with continuing the mission of Jesus, spreading the gospel and making disciples of all nations (Matthew 28:19-20).

3. Unity in Diversity: Jesus' teachings promote unity among diverse peoples, reflecting the inclusive nature of God's kingdom (Galatians 3:28).

4. Ethical Transformation: The ethical and moral teachings of Jesus continue to shape personal and societal values, promoting justice, compassion, and integrity (Matthew 5:16).

5. Eschatological Hope: The global spread of the gospel is part of God's redemptive plan, leading to the fulfillment of His kingdom purposes and the ultimate reconciliation of all things (Acts 1:8).

Comprehensive Commentary

Matthew Henry comments: "Isaiah's vision of a light to the Gentiles finds its fulfillment in the global mission of Jesus Christ. His teachings have brought salvation to the ends of the earth, transforming lives and societies. The Church, empowered by the Holy Spirit, continues this mission, spreading the light of the gospel to all nations."

John Calvin, in his Institutes of the Christian Religion, writes: "The universal scope of the gospel, as foretold by Isaiah, is realized in the teachings and mission of Jesus Christ. The Church is called to be a light to the nations, bearing witness to the salvation found in Christ alone. This mission is both a privilege and a responsibility, grounded in the assurance of God's presence and power."

Conclusion

The global impact of Jesus' teachings and the fulfillment of Isaiah's vision for the nations demonstrate the transformative power of the gospel. Jesus' command to spread the message of salvation to all nations has led to the establishment of a global Church, united in mission and purpose. The teachings of Jesus continue to shape ethical and moral standards, promote unity and justice, and inspire believers to carry the light of the gospel to every corner of the earth.

This chapter has explored the profound connections between Isaiah's vision and the global mission of Jesus, offering an expository study and comprehensive commentary on their fulfillment. As we embrace this mission, we participate in God's redemptive plan, bringing the message of hope and salvation to a world in need.

CHAPTER 07

THE FULFILLMENT OF GOD'S PROMISE

Jesus Christ stands at the center of the Christian faith, embodying the fulfillment of God's promises as prophesied in the book of Isaiah. His life, teachings, death, and resurrection are not only historical events but also profound theological truths that affirm His divinity and eternal role as Savior. This conclusion reflects on the journey through the prophetic words of Isaiah and their fulfillment in Jesus, enriching our faith and deepening our appreciation for the divine plan revealed in Scripture.

The Prophetic Foundation

The prophecies of Isaiah provide a detailed and compelling vision of the Messiah. Isaiah 7:14 speaks of a virgin giving birth to a son named Immanuel, meaning "God with us." Isaiah 9:6-7 foretells a child born to establish an everlasting kingdom of justice and righteousness. Isaiah 53 vividly describes the Suffering Servant, who would bear the sins of many and secure salvation through His sacrificial death.

These prophecies lay a foundation for understanding the mission and identity of Jesus Christ. They highlight God's plan to redeem humanity through the coming of the Messiah, a plan that unfolds with precision and divine intent in the New Testament.

The Fulfillment in Jesus Christ

Jesus' life and ministry reflect the fulfillment of Isaiah's prophecies. His birth to the Virgin Mary fulfills the sign of Immanuel. His teachings, such as the Sermon on the Mount and the parables, reveal the nature of God's kingdom and the ethical standards of its citizens. His miracles demonstrate His divine authority and compassion, aligning with Isaiah's vision of a healer and restorer.

The crucifixion of Jesus is the pinnacle of His role as the Suffering Servant. He was "pierced for our transgressions" and "crushed for our iniquities" (Isaiah 53:5). His resurrection from the dead signifies His victory over sin and death, affirming His identity as the Son of God and the source of eternal life.

The Great Commission and Global Impact

The Great Commission, recorded in Matthew 28:19-20, commands Jesus' followers to spread the gospel to all nations. This universal mission reflects Isaiah's vision of a light for the Gentiles and salvation reaching the ends of the earth (Isaiah 49:6). The teachings of Jesus have transformed individuals, communities, and cultures worldwide, promoting values of love, justice, and compassion.

The global impact of Jesus' teachings is evident in the growth of the Church, the spread of Christian ethics, and the ongoing mission to bring the message of salvation to all people. Believers are called to continue this mission, empowered by the Holy Spirit and assured of Jesus' continual presence.

Theological Implications and Enrichment of Faith

Understanding the connections between Isaiah's prophecies and their fulfillment in Jesus Christ enriches our faith. It provides a deeper appreciation for the coherence and continuity of God's redemptive plan. These connections affirm the reliability of Scripture, the sovereignty of God, and the centrality of Jesus Christ in salvation history.

As believers, recognizing Jesus as the fulfillment of God's promises invites us to live in the light of His teachings, embodying the values of His kingdom and participating in His mission. It encourages us to trust in God's faithfulness, knowing that His promises are true and His plan is perfect.

Conclusion

Jesus Christ, as prophesied in Isaiah, embodies the fulfillment of God's promise to humanity. His life, teachings, death, and resurrection are a testament to His divinity and eternal role as Savior. Understanding these connections enriches our faith and provides a deeper appreciation for the divine plan laid out in the Scriptures.

As we reflect on the prophetic words of Isaiah and their fulfillment in Jesus, we are called to a renewed commitment to follow Him, share His message, and live out His teachings in our daily lives. This journey through the Scriptures reveals the profound and unchanging truth that in Jesus Christ, God's promises are fulfilled, and His salvation is made available to all.

In Him, we find hope, purpose, and the assurance of eternal life. Let us continue to seek a deeper understanding of His word, a closer relationship with Him, and a faithful response to His call, knowing that He is with us always, to the very end of the age.

REFERENCES

Holy Bible, New International Version

Scholarly Articles and Theological Texts

1. Brueggemann, Walter. Isaiah 1-39 and Isaiah 40-66. Westminster John Knox Press, 1998.

- These volumes provide an in-depth commentary on the book of Isaiah, offering critical insights and theological reflections on its prophecies.

2. Goldingay, John. The Theology of the Book of Isaiah. IVP Academic, 2014.

- This text explores the overarching themes and theological messages of Isaiah, including the messianic prophecies and their fulfillment in the New Testament.

3. Motyer, J. Alec. The Prophecy of Isaiah: An Introduction and Commentary. InterVarsity Press, 1993.

- Motyer's work provides a comprehensive commentary on Isaiah, with particular emphasis on the messianic prophecies and their significance in Christian theology.

4. Calvin, John. Institutes of the Christian Religion. Translated by Henry Beveridge, 1845.

- Calvin's foundational work in Reformed theology offers valuable insights into the fulfillment of Old Testament prophecies in Jesus Christ.

5. Henry, Matthew. Matthew Henry's Commentary on the Whole Bible.

- This classic commentary provides verse-by-verse explanations and theological reflections on both the Old and New Testaments, including the book of Isaiah and the Gospels.

6. Nolland, John. The Gospel of Matthew: A Commentary on the Greek Text. Eerdmans, 2005.

- Nolland's scholarly work offers an in-depth analysis of the Gospel of Matthew, including the Great Commission and its implications for Christian mission.

7. Green, Joel B., McKnight, Scot, and Marshall, I. Howard. Dictionary of Jesus and the Gospels. InterVarsity Press, 1992.

- This comprehensive dictionary provides detailed entries on the life, teachings, and theological significance of Jesus, including His fulfillment of Old Testament prophecies.

8. Keener, Craig S. The Gospel of John: A Commentary. Baker Academic, 2003.

- Keener's commentary offers a thorough examination of the Gospel of John, including its Christological themes and references to Isaiah's prophecies.

9. Wright, N.T. Jesus and the Victory of God. Fortress Press, 1996.

- Wright's work explores the historical and theological aspects of Jesus' life and mission, with a focus on His fulfillment of Old Testament expectations.

10. Carson, D.A., and Moo, Douglas J. An Introduction to the New Testament. Zondervan, 2005.

- This introductory text provides an overview of the New Testament, including the relationship between its writings and the Old Testament prophecies.

These references provide a comprehensive foundation for understanding the fulfillment of Isaiah's prophecies in Jesus Christ and the ongoing impact of His teachings on Christian ethics and behavior.

In the quiet moments of reflection that followed the tumultuous journey of the gold rush, John and Emily found themselves sitting by the flickering campfire, gazing into its embers as the stars painted patterns in the night sky. It was in these moments that they began to grasp the profound truth that the true value of their experience wasn't solely in the pursuit of gold.

APPENDICES

Appendix A: Key Messianic Prophecies in Isaiah

1. Isaiah 7:14 - The Virgin Birth

- "Therefore the Lord himself will give you a sign: The virgin will conceive and give birth to a son, and will call him Immanuel."

- Fulfillment: Matthew 1:23 identifies Jesus' birth as the fulfillment of this prophecy, emphasizing His divine nature as "God with us."

2. Isaiah 9:6-7 - The Titles of the Messiah

- "For to us a child is born, to us a son is given, and the government will be on his shoulders. And he will be called Wonderful Counselor, Mighty God, Everlasting Father, Prince of Peace."

- Fulfillment: These titles are reflected in the New Testament descriptions of Jesus, affirming His divinity and eternal reign (Luke 1:32-33).

3. Isaiah 53 - The Suffering Servant

- "But he was pierced for our transgressions, he was crushed for our iniquities; the punishment that brought us peace was on him, and by his wounds we are healed."

- Fulfillment: The New Testament portrays Jesus as the Suffering Servant who takes on the sins of humanity, especially in 1 Peter 2:24 and Philippians 2:8.

4. Isaiah 42:1-4 - The Chosen Servant

- "Here is my servant, whom I uphold, my chosen one in whom I delight; I will put my Spirit on him, and he will bring justice to the nations."

- Fulfillment: This prophecy is reflected in the baptism of Jesus, where the Holy Spirit descends upon Him, and God's voice affirms His Sonship (Matthew 3:16-17).

Appendix B: Theological Concepts Related to Jesus' Divinity in Isaiah

1. Immanuel - "God with Us"

- The concept of Immanuel in Isaiah 7:14 speaks to the incarnation of God in Jesus Christ, signifying God's presence with humanity in a tangible way.

2. The Role of the Servant

- Isaiah presents the Messiah as the Servant of the Lord who carries out God's will through humility, suffering, and eventual exaltation (Isaiah 42, 49, 52-53). This Servant is both divine and human, fulfilling God's redemptive plan.

3. The Suffering Messiah

- Isaiah 53 introduces the concept of a suffering Messiah, a theological foundation for understanding Jesus' atoning death. The suffering Servant motif underscores the divine plan for redemption through sacrifice.

4. Eschatological Hope

- Isaiah's prophecies often point to a future eschatological fulfillment, where the Messiah will establish an eternal kingdom characterized by justice and peace (Isaiah 9:7). This eschatological hope is fulfilled in Jesus' second coming as described in Revelation.

5. Messianic Titles

- Titles such as "Mighty God" and "Prince of Peace" (Isaiah 9:6) are essential for understanding Jesus' identity as both divine and sovereign. These titles affirm the Messiah's role in establishing God's kingdom on earth.

Appendix C: Comparative Analysis of Old and New Testament Fulfillments

1. Isaiah 7:14 and Matthew 1:23

- Isaiah: The prophecy of a virgin birth points to a miraculous sign of God's intervention.

- Matthew: The birth of Jesus to the Virgin Mary directly fulfills this prophecy, emphasizing the supernatural nature of Jesus' origin.

2. Isaiah 9:6-7 and Luke 1:32-33

- Isaiah: The prophecy outlines the eternal reign of a divine king from David's line.

- Luke: The angel Gabriel's announcement to Mary confirms Jesus as the heir to David's throne, who will reign forever.

3. Isaiah 53 and 1 Peter 2:24

- Isaiah: The Suffering Servant bears the sins of many, offering healing through His wounds.

- 1 Peter: Peter interprets Jesus' suffering and death as the fulfillment of Isaiah's prophecy, highlighting its redemptive significance.

4. Isaiah 42:1-4 and Matthew 3:16-17

- Isaiah: The Servant is chosen by God and endowed with the Spirit to bring justice to the nations.

- Matthew: Jesus' baptism scene echoes this prophecy, as the Spirit descends on Him and God affirms Him as His beloved Son.

Appendix D: Historical and Cultural Context of Isaiah's Prophecies

1. Historical Background

- Isaiah prophesied during the 8th century BCE, a time of political turmoil and spiritual decline in Israel and Judah. His messages often addressed both immediate political concerns and future messianic hopes.

2. Cultural Significance

- The use of royal and Servant imagery in Isaiah reflects the cultural expectations of a coming ruler who would restore Israel and bring peace. These images were deeply embedded in Jewish messianic hopes, which Jesus fulfills in the New Testament.

3. Prophetic Literature

- Isaiah is part of the prophetic tradition, which often used symbolic language, metaphors, and visions to convey divine messages. Understanding these literary forms is crucial for interpreting the messianic prophecies related to Jesus.

Appendix E: Glossary of Key Terms

1. Immanuel: "God with us," a name used in Isaiah 7:14 to signify the divine presence in the Messiah.

2. Messiah: Anointed one; the promised deliverer of Israel, fulfilled in Jesus Christ.

3. Servant of the Lord: A term used in Isaiah to describe the Messiah, who fulfills God's redemptive plan through suffering and exaltation.

4. Eschatology: The study of the end times, including the final events of history as they relate to God's ultimate plan for creation.

5. Atonement: The reconciliation between God and humanity, accomplished through the sacrificial death of Jesus.

6. Trinitarian Theology: The Christian doctrine of the Trinity, which describes God as three persons in one essence—Father, Son, and Holy Spirit.

Appendix F: Bibliography

A list of scholarly references and sources used in the development of this book, including theological commentaries, historical studies, and biblical exegesis related to the divinity of Jesus in the book of Isaiah.

These appendices provide additional resources and context for readers to deepen their understanding of the themes explored in "The Divinity of Jesus in the Book of Isaiah" by Dr. Maxwell Shimba. They are designed to enhance the study of Isaiah's prophecies and their fulfillment in Jesus Christ, offering tools for further reflection and research.

STUDY GUIDE AND REFLECTION QUESTIONS

This study guide is designed to help readers engage more deeply with the content of "The Divinity of Jesus in the Book of Isaiah" by Dr. Maxwell Shimba. The reflection questions are intended to stimulate thought, discussion, and personal application of the material presented in each chapter. These questions can be used individually or in group settings to facilitate a richer understanding of the themes and messages explored in the book.

Chapter 1: The Prophetic Foundation in Isaiah

Study Questions:

1. How does Isaiah 7:14's prophecy about Immanuel contribute to our understanding of Jesus' divine nature?

2. What is the significance of the virgin birth in the context of Isaiah's prophecy and its fulfillment in the New Testament?

3. In what ways does the prophecy in Isaiah 7:14 provide hope for both the ancient audience and modern readers?

4. How do the Old Testament prophecies strengthen the foundation of Christian faith in the divinity of Jesus?

Reflection Questions:

1. Reflect on the name "Immanuel" and its implications for your personal relationship with God. How does knowing that "God is with us" impact your daily life?

2. Consider the miraculous nature of the virgin birth. How does this event challenge or affirm your understanding of God's power and sovereignty?

3. How can the fulfillment of Isaiah's prophecies in the New Testament deepen your trust in the reliability of Scripture?

Chapter 2: A Child is Born – The Titles and Attributes of Jesus

Study Questions:

1. What do the titles "Wonderful Counselor," "Mighty God," "Everlasting Father," and "Prince of Peace" reveal about Jesus' identity and mission?

2. How do these titles, given in Isaiah 9:6-7, relate to the expectations of the Messiah in the Old Testament?

3. How is the promise of an everlasting kingdom in Isaiah 9:7 fulfilled in the life and work of Jesus Christ?

Reflection Questions:

1. Which of the titles attributed to Jesus in Isaiah 9:6-7 resonates most with you, and why?

2. Reflect on the concept of Jesus as "Mighty God." How does this understanding influence your worship and relationship with Him?

3. How can the peace that Jesus, the "Prince of Peace," brings be manifested in your personal life and interactions with others?

Chapter 3: The Suffering Servant – Isaiah 53 and the Atonement

Study Questions:

1. How does Isaiah 53 describe the Messiah's role as the Suffering Servant, and what are the key aspects of His suffering?

2. In what ways does the New Testament connect Jesus' crucifixion with the prophecies in Isaiah 53?

3. What theological significance does the concept of substitutionary atonement hold in Christian doctrine, based on Isaiah 53?

Reflection Questions:

1. Reflect on the nature of Jesus' suffering as described in Isaiah 53. How does this understanding affect your view of sin and redemption?

2. How does the knowledge of Jesus bearing your iniquities influence your approach to repentance and forgiveness?

3. In what ways can you live out the reality of Jesus' atonement in your daily life, particularly in how you interact with others?

Chapter 4: The Great Commission – Spreading the Gospel

Study Questions:

1. How does the Great Commission in Matthew 28:19-20 fulfill Isaiah's vision of salvation reaching the nations (Isaiah 49:6)?

2. What are the key components of the Great Commission, and how do they relate to the mission of the Church today?

3. How does Jesus' promise to be with His disciples "to the very end of the age" provide assurance and motivation for carrying out the Great Commission?

Reflection Questions:

1. Reflect on your role in fulfilling the Great Commission. How can you be more active in sharing the gospel in your community?

2. Consider the global scope of the Great Commission. How can you support or participate in mission work, both locally and internationally?

3. How does the assurance of Jesus' presence empower you to overcome challenges and fears in spreading the gospel?

Chapter 5: The Global Impact of Jesus' Teachings and Isaiah's Vision for the Nations

Study Questions:

1. How has Jesus' teaching influenced global ethics, morality, and culture, particularly in fulfilling Isaiah's vision for the nations?

2. What is the significance of the Church's role in spreading the light of Christ to the Gentiles, as prophesied in Isaiah 49:6?

3. How do the teachings of Jesus continue to shape the mission and vision of the Church today, especially in diverse cultural contexts?

Reflection Questions:

1. Reflect on the ways Jesus' teachings have impacted your personal ethics and behavior. How can you better align your life with His teachings?

2. Consider the global reach of the gospel. How does understanding the fulfillment of Isaiah's vision inspire you to be more involved in the global mission of the Church?

3. How can you contribute to the ongoing work of spreading the light of Christ to all nations, in your local context and beyond?

Chapter 6: The Divinity of Jesus in the Book of Isaiah

Study Questions:

1. What evidence does the book of Isaiah provide for the divinity of Jesus Christ, and how is this fulfilled in the New Testament?

2. How do the titles and prophecies in Isaiah reinforce the understanding of Jesus as the divine Messiah?

3. How does the connection between Isaiah's prophecies and the New Testament accounts deepen the theological understanding of Jesus' divinity?

Reflection Questions:

1. Reflect on the ways in which Isaiah's prophecies have strengthened your faith in Jesus as the divine Messiah. How does this understanding impact your worship and devotion?

2. Consider the significance of the prophetic fulfillment in Jesus. How does recognizing these connections enhance your appreciation of the Bible as a unified and coherent revelation?

3. How can you incorporate the truths about Jesus' divinity into your daily spiritual practice, prayer life, and witness to others?

This study guide and the accompanying reflection questions are designed to help you engage more deeply with the themes and teachings of "The Divinity of Jesus in the Book of Isaiah" by Dr. Maxwell Shimba. By reflecting on these questions, you will be able to apply the insights from the book to your personal faith journey and to your broader understanding of Christian doctrine and mission.